BIBLIOTHECA INDO BUDDHICA NO. 39

The Mission of Wang Hiuen Ts'e in India

Written in French by

M. SYLVAIN LEVI

Translated from the Original French by

S. P. CHATTERJEE

Edited by

B. C. LAW

SRI SATGURU PUBLICATIONS
DELHI—INDIA

Published by :
SRI SATGURU PUBLICATIONS
a Division of :
INDIAN BOOKS CENTRE
Indological and Oriental Publishers
40/5, Shakti Nagar,
Delhi–110007
(INDIA)

First Edition—Calcutta 1967

Second Edition–Delhi 1987

I.S.B.N.—81-7030-127-0

Printed in :
Kiran Mudran Kendra
A-38/2, Maya Puri, Phase I,
New Delhi-110064.

EDITOR'S NOTE

The travels of Wang Hiuen-ts'e written in Chinese and translated into French by M. Sylvain Levi are interesting. To make his travels known to a large section of people, Dr. S. P. Chatterjee undertook to translate into English from the original French the account of his travels. We are really thankful to him for the task so ably done by him.

The Chinese envoys were able to pass through Tibet and its dependency Nepal as allied countries while on their wny to the court of Harṣa in A.D. 643-45. Both these kingdoms willingly sent troops to rescue Wang Hiuen-ts'e. After Harṣa's death the troops of Tibet and Nepal acted together in favour of Wang Hiuen-ts'e, the Chinese envoy, and against the usurper of Harṣa's throne. Harṣa maintained diplomatic intercourse with China. A Brahmin envoy was sent to the king of China in 641 A.D. by Harṣa. He returned in A.D. 643 accompanied by a Chinese mission. This mission remained long in India and did not go back to China until 645 A.D. In 646 A.D. Wang Hiuen-ts'e was sent by his king as the head of a new mission to India with an escort of 30 horsemen. Arjuna or Aruṇāśva usurped the throne and took the field against the Chinese mission. Then ensued massacre of the members of the escort and the plunder of the property of the mission. Wang Hiuen-ts'e and his colleague escaped to Nepal by night. Wang with his small army succeeded in storming the city of Tirhut. Arjuna fled. Wang brought the usurper as a prisoner to China and was promoted for his services.

Wang once more visited the scene of his adventures, being sent by the king of China in A.D. 657, to offer robes to Buddhist holy places. He entered India through Nepal by the Lasha road which was then open and used by Buddhist pilgrims. After paying his respects at Vaiśālī, Bodh-Gayā and other holy places, he returned home through Kapiśa or northern Afganistan by the Hindukush and Pamir route.

I have added foot notes wherever needed to make the subject matter intelligible to scholars and laymen alike.

Like the Travels of Fa-hien and Hiouen Tsang, who visited India in the 5th and 7th centries A.D., I believe the account of Wang Hiuen-ts'e's travels will very be useful.

43 KAILAS BOSE STREET,
CALCUTTA 6.
January, 1967

B. C. Law

CONTENTS

WANG HIUEN-TS'E AND HIS MISSIONS IN INDIA

I

The name of Wang Hiuen-ts'e[1] is not altogether unknown to Indologists. The Chinese references to India, translated by Pauthier and Stanislas Julien, have made known the adventures of this person, contemporary of Hiouen-Tsang, who left China as a simple carrier of official presents with an escort of thirty cavalry. He played the role of an improvised diplomat and general, succeeded in uniting Tibet and Nepal against Hindustan, and brought to his emperor a king of Magadha as prisoner. He had written accounts of his travels, but they are lost. Fortunately, a few extracts have been preserved in *Fa-iouen-tchou-lin.* This famous encyclopædia of Buddhism, compiled by Tao-cheu and completed in 668, refers to *Tchoung-T'ien-tchouhing ki,* 'Account of travels in central India', by Wang Hiuen-ts'e as one of the authoritative works. That was in one volume, divided into ten chapters. Elsewhere in the book this account is mentioned under slightly different titles : *'Wang Hiuen-ts'e hing tchoan'* i.e., 'Account of a travel of Wang Hiuen-ts'e ; *'Si-kouo hing tchoan'* i.e., 'Account of a travel in the kingdoms of the West' ; *'Si-iu hing tchoan'* i.e., 'Account of a travel in the countries of the West'. It is chiefly from the records of Wang Hiuen-ts'e and those of Hiouen-Tsang that an official account was prepared in 666 known as *Si-iu-tchi* (also called *Si-kouo-tchi*). It contained one hundred chapters, sixty texts, forty maps and charts. I have collected and included in the present work the writings of Wang Hiuen-ts'e as found in *Fa-ioueu-tchou-lin* and collected at the same time other relevant information. I have translated also several extracts from *Si-iu-tchi* which appeared to me to be of some interest to Indologists. The rare fragments of *Tchoung T'ien-tchou-hing ki* make us regret further the loss of the book which is considered as full of wonders as that of Hiouen-Tsang. The author was also acquainted with the art of observing and

---

1 Sylvain Levi's article entitled "Les Missions de Wang Hiuen-ts'e dans l' Inde" appears in *Journal Asiatique,* 1900. V. A. Smith has given a wrong reference to its English translation in the *Indian Antiquary,* 1911, pp. 111 ff.—B. C. Law.

taking precise notes of things he observed, and he was less troubled by dogmas and theology. It was as a statesman that he visited the courts and convents of India and the neighbouring countries.

Before taking the charge of a mission Wang Hiuen-ts'e was attached second-in-command to the mission of Li-I-Piao who left for India in the third month of the year 643. Li-I-Piao had borne the exalted title of *tch'ao-san-ta-fou* and that of *wei wei*; Wang had acted before as the chief administrator at Hoang-choei in the district of Ioung. The escort consisted of 22 persons. The mission had the object of accompanying to India a Brahmin, an official guest of the Empire, or according to the *History of the T'ang dynasty* to return to the king Harṣa Śilāditya[1] an answer from the emperor. The Brahmin was undoubtedly an ambassador of this king. After travelling for nine months, they arrived in Magadha[2] in the tenth month of the year 643. They stayed for a considerable time in India, mainly for religious purposes. In 645 at the end of the first month they reached Rājagṛha[3], ascended the Gṛdhrakūṭa[4], and left there an inscription. A

---

1 Sylvain Levi calls Harṣa Śilāditya which is very rerely used. In the Maukhari coins Śilāditya is used for Harṣa—Cf. R. K. Mookerjee, *Harsha*, p. 16 f. n. 2. —B. C. Law.

2 Magadha corresponded to the modern district of Patna in the Buddha's time. Magadha or Madhyamaṇḍala was supposed to be situated in the centre of Jambudvīpa or the continent of India according to the Siamese books. It is generally regarded as answering to central Bihar It is called Makata by the Burmese and Siamese; Mo-ki-to by the Chinese and Makala Kokf by the Japanese. Rapson says that Magadha or southērn Bihar comprises the districts of Gaya and Patna (*CHI.*, I, p. 166). It should be placed to the west of Aṅga (modern Bhagalpur) being separated from the latter kingdom by the river Campā (Cf. H. C. Raychaudhuri, *Political History*, p. 53).—B C.L.

3. It was the ancient capital of Magadha. Here the two chief diselples of the Buddha, Sāriputta and Moggallāna were converted by him. Its importance in the history of Buddhism, is very great. It was from this place the Buddha undertook his last journey to Kusinārā (B. C. Law, *The Magadhas in Ancient India*, *RAS Publication* No. 24; *Rājagriha in Ancient Literature in MASI.*, No. 58)—B.C.L.

4 The Most famous of the mountains encircling Rājagriha was Gṛdhrakūṭa or Gijjhakūṭa peak (Ki-tche-kiu). It was so called either because it was shaped like a vulture's beak or because it was frequented by vultures (*Suttanipāta commy.*, p. 413) —B. C. L.

fortnight afterwards they reached Mahābodhi[1] and there inscribed an account of their visit. They must have passed by Nepal either while going or on returning, where the king Narendradeva received Li-I-Piao warmly.[2]

On returning to China, Wang Hiuen-ts'e did not delay in taking again the route to the west. In the year 646 (if the account of *Ma-Toan-lin*[3] is correct) *Wang Hiuen-Ts'e*, who received the title of 'Chief of Guard and Keeper of the Records' (*iou-wei-choai-fou tch' ang cheu*), was entrusted to lead a mission to Magadha. He got as his second officer *Tsiang Cheu-Jenn* and an escort of thirty cavalry. But when he was on his way, the king Harṣa Śilāditya died; his minister *Na-fou-ti O-lo-na-choen*[4] usurped the throne, broke off with China, and took him as enemy. The escort was annihilated, the treasure was plundered. The envoy and his chief assistant fled at night. Nepal was not far away; Wang Hiuen-ts'e remembered the reception given to the mission

---

1 The lofty temple of Bodh-Gayā continued to be known by the name of Mahābodhi even as late as the year 1877 (Cunningham, *Mahābodhi*, p. 2). The Bodh-Gayā temple was known to Hiuen Tsang as Mahābodhi (*Mo-ho-pu-ti*) vihāra and the monastery by the name of Mahābodhi saṅghārāma (Beal, *Buddhist Records*, II, p. 133). The name of Mahābodhi also occurs in the inscription of Keśava recording the installation of a Caumukha Mahādeva during the reign of king Dharmapāla. The name Mahābodhi was used by all Chinese pilgrims who visited the place in the 7th century A.D.

2 See my *Notes sur la chronologie du Nepal* in *Journal Asiatique*, 1894, p. 68 (where the date of the period Tcheng-Koan is to be corrected as follows : 627-649).

3 *Notice sur l'Inde* translated by St. Julien in *Journal Asiatique* 1847, 2 (reproduced in *Indian Antiquary*, IX, p. 20). But *Tsi-Kou-Kin-fou-tao-loen-heng* reports that Li-I-Piao returned in 647.

4 The conjecture that I made (*Journ. Asiat.*, 1894, p. 388) on the meaning of *Na-fou-ti* (*senāpati*) is to be discarded. The letter '*fou*' should represent a mute letter ended by an 'u' or 'o'. *Fou-ti* cannot mean 'pati'. Besides, the inscription reported by M. Chavannes (*Revue de l'Histoire des Religions*, XXXIV, p 28) corroborates the accuracy of the form given in the *Annals of the T'ang*, but it suggests another explanation. Under the title : *Po-lo-men ti-na-fou-ti*, if the letter *ti* following *po-la-men* has its ideographic value, and if it means "emperor of the Brahmins" ; it is hardly justifiable that the same letter a little later will have simple phonetic value. It will be rash to choose between the two possible solutions : firstly the emperor of the Brahmins, the emperor of *Na-fou*, the king *Kouo-wang*) *O-la-na-choen* ; secondly the king of the kingdom of *Ti-na-fou-ti* (*bhukti* ?) of the Brahmins (of India) *O-lo-na-choen*.

of Li-I-Piao in which he was also a member. Narendradeva was still ruling in that country. Across Nepal there was Tibet, where the king Srong-tsan Gam-po was an ally of China, and had married in 641 a princess of the Imperial family. The two states lent their soldiers to Wang Hiuen-ts'e. At the head of 1200 Tibetans and 7,000 Nepalese cavalry he marched on Magadha, defeated the Indian troops, captured the capital, seized the king and took him triumphantly to China. Wang Hiuen-ts'e and his prisoner arrived on *Keng tzeu* day in the fifth month of 648; the envoy became famous at once and was promoted to the rank of *tch'ao-san-ta-fou.* Later on, when the mausoleum of the emperor Tai-tsoung, who died in 649, was built, the statue of *O-lo-na-choen* wns erected on the street leading to the tomb, along with the statues of Srong-tsan Gam-po, the kings of Kou-tches and of Kao-tchang etc.[1]

The texts on this mission are explicit; they are also corroborated by other sources. In the account of Tibet incorporated in the *History of the T'ang dynasty* we find the following passage: "In the 22nd year Tcheng-koan (648) the royal envoy Wang Hiuen-ts'e, who was charged with a mission in the western countries, was plundered in central India. Tibet had helped him with an army of brave soldiers who fought under the command of Wang Hiuen-ts'e. They attacked India and inflicted a crushing defeat, and despatched messengers to the emperor announcing their victory." The 'Account of Nepal' in the same history (book CCXXI), after mentioning the visit of Li-I-Piao, says "As soon as Wang Hiuen-ts'e was maltreated by the Indians, Nepal and Tibet came to his rescue and gave him military help. The combined armies attacked the Indian army and won a decisive victory."[2] It is also mentioned there in a chronological order that an ambassador was sent to China in 651 by Narendradeva. We cannot, therefore, attach any importance to the passage in the book *Siu-kao seng-tchoan* (chap. IV, p. 106) quoted

---

1 See Chavannes, *Les Inscriptions Chinoises de Bodh-Gaya* in *Revue de l'Histoire des Religions*, 1896, p. 28; and Bushell, *Early History of Tibet*, in *J.R.A.S.*, n.s. XII, p. 528, note 16.

2 S. Levi *Notes sur la chronologie du Nepal* in *Journ. Asiat*, 1894, 2, p. 68.

by Mr. Chavannes[1] which refers to the death of Śilāditya sometime in 655. Besides, that passage is reported from the 'Biography of Hiouen-tsang' by Hoei-li.

The Biography of Hiouen-tsang should not prevail upon so many precise texts; for an estimate of its value it should be enough to remember the vicissitudes through which it passed before its publication; it remained incomplete and fragmentary after the death of its author. "It was full of errors, contradictory and incomplete statements" (*Song Kao seng tchoan*, as quoted by Julien, Preface, p. LXXIX). Ien-ts'ong, who put it in order, "made the necessary changes, improved on the original composition, corrected the mistakes, and cleared up the obscure statements." Ien-ts'ong, like Hoei-li, was not so much interested in the Indian chronology. Both of them wanted to present to the public a book of edification. Mañjuśrī had predicted sometime in 644 the death of Śilāditya ten years after. Śilāditya was to have died ten years later. Mañjuśrī, Hoei-li and Ien-ts'ong might agree with historians, in case of need, because in supporting ambiguous and unintelligible statements of oracles it is permissible to interpret the prediction as follows: "Ten years hence the emperor Śilāditya would die and India would be a victim of dreadful disorder; and the wicked persons would wage relentless war."

Mañjuśrī, according to Hoei-li, wanted to press for the departure of his master who was delaying to go back to his country. The announcement of this death, which was to befall in ten years, was enough to force a decision. "As he prolonged his sojourn and was not keen to return", says the biographer, "Mañjuśrī announced the approaching death (of the king Śilāditya) for forcing a decision. The fulfilment of the prophecy, without making any violent departure from the text, admits of the following translation." By the end of the period Iong-hoei (650-655) the king Śilāditya having died, India, in conformity with the prediction, became a victim to the horrors of famine, Wang Hiuen-ts'e, whom the emperor of China sent to India as

1 I-tsing, *Les religieux éminents*.........trans, Chavannes, p. 19. note 2.

ambassador, was a witness to the calamity.[1] It appears, therefore, that the author had in view a third visit of Wang Hiuen-ts'e to India.

In 657 A.D. Wang Hiuen-ts'e by an Imperial Order was sent to the western countries in the capacity of *Wei-tchang-cheu.* This time the mission was to offer a *kasāya* (yellow robe) to the holy places. It had also the object of bringing back to China the mystic *Hiuen-tchao,* whom Wang Hiuen-ts'e had met previously in India and described him as one of the most virtuous men of the time. We know something of the stages of this journey.

In 657 A.D. Wang Hiuen-ts'e went once again through Nepal; in 659 A.D. he was in the kingdom of *Fo-li-che*; in 660 A.D. he was in the convent of Mahābodhi where the Vihārasvāmin Śilanāga treated him with great honour; a procession of monks accompanied him in tears when he left the convent on the first day of the tenth month in the year 660. In 661 he was in Kapiśā[2], carrying out simultaneously religious and political missions just before returning to China. He had to visit on his way Vaiśālī[3] and to witness a grand show given in his honour by the emperor of India.

---

1 A printing mistake in the translation made by Julien has again confused this question. The French text says : "A la fin de la periode Yong-hoe (650), le roi Kiaï-Ji (Śilāditya) mourat en effet" The year 650, the beginning of the peiiod, is, by mistake, indicated as the end. Cunningham (*Ancient Geography of India*, pp. 569-70), who made use of the translation of Julien without being able to verify it, has given reasons which led the biographer to alter the facts, and he refused to admit his evidence.

2 It is Chinese *kia-pi-shi.* It is the Capissa of Pliny and the Caphusa of Solinus. According to Ptolemy it was situated 155 miles north-east from Kabul. Julien considers this place to have occupied the Panjshir and the Tagao valleys in the northern border of Kohistan. For further details vide Watters, *On Yuan Chwang*, I, p. 122 ; Beal, *Buddhist Records of the Western World*, I, 54 ff—B. C. L.

3 Cunningham identifies Vaiśālī with Basarh in the Muzaffapur district in Tirhut (*ASR.*, I, 55-56 ; XVI, p. 6). Vivien de St. Martin is of the same opinion, T. W. Rhys Davids differs from them and says that it was somewhere in Tirhut (*Buddhist India*, p. 41). W. Hoey tries to establish its identity with Cherand in the Chapra or Saran district (*JASB.*, 1900, Vol. LXIX, Pt. I, pp. 78-80, 83). V. A. Smith is of the opinion that Vaiśālī may be identified with Basarh (*JRAS.*, 1902, p. 267, n. 3). The Archæological excavations carried out by T. Bloch on

The texts do dot help us in following Wang Hiuen-ts'e much further. It is very likely that on his return he began to write his book entitled 'Account of the Voyage' in his leisure time, which was published before the compilation of *Si-iu-tchi* in 666 A.D. His example must have inspired the members of his family; his nephew, *T-che-hong* left as a pilgrim for the country of the Buddha. He went by sea *via* Śrī Bhoja, Ceylon, Harikela[1], and lived for ten years in Central India, visiting sacred places and studying sacred texts at Nālandā.

The campaign of Wang Hiuen-ts'e in Magadha as given in the History of T'ang

The *History of the T'ang dynasty* in both of its redactions has incorporated a short account of the second mission in Magadha which ended with the defeat and capture of the usurper *O-lo-na-choen. Ma Toan-lin* and *Pien-i-tien* have reproduced literally the account, published in the *New History.* The translations of Julien and Pauthier have made these accounts long accessible to Indologists. The ancient history, more brief, has so far been neglected. It was mainly with the help of that book that we could fix with precision the date of return of Wang Hiuen-ts'e. The translations that I give below from the two texts will facilitate a comparison and rectification.

---

the site have decisively proved this identification, B. C. Law, *Vaiśālī in Ancient Literature* published in the *Homage to Vaiśālī* (Ed. by Jagadis Chandra Mathur and Yogendra Mishra, pp. 30-31)—B.C.L.

1 *Harikela* was an eastern country. Some have identified it with Vaṅga (*IHQ.*, II, 322; *Ibid.*, XIX, 220). According to some it was the coast land between Samataṭa and Orissa (*History of Bengal*, Dacca University, I, 134-35) while others hold that it may be identified with some portions of Backerganj and Noakhali districts (Paul, *Early History of Bengal*, I, pp. iii-iv). Some go so far to identify it with Chittagong and with a tract roughly covering the southern part of Tipperah district (*IHQ.*, XX, 5; *Proceedings of the Indian History Congress*, VII, 1944). Harikela (*O-li-ki-lo* or *A-li-ki-lo*) was visited by two Chinese priests according to I-tsing (*A record of the Buddhist religion*,Tr. by Takakusu, 1896, p. xlvi). Both these priests came to Harikela by the southern sea-route. It was an inland country, situated some 40 yojanas to the north Tāmralipti. It lay wholly on the west of the river Meghnā. The *Karpuramañjarī* (Nirṇayasāgara Ed. p. 13) includes it in eastern India (Cf. *Indian Culture*, XII, 88 ff.)—B.C Law.

New History of the T'ang Dynasty
Chap. 221, 1st part (India)

In the 22nd year (*Tcheng-koan*) (648) Wang Hiuen-ts'e who was *iou-wei-choai-fou, tch'ang-cheu* (the chief of the guard of the right and keeper of records) was sent as an envoy to this country (*T'ien-tchou* = 'India') with Tsiang Cheu-Jean as his chief assistant. Before their arrival *Chi-lo-i-to* (Śilāditya) died; the kingdom fell in anarchy. *Na-fou-ti O-lo-na-choen*, the minister, captured the throne. He placed the army in the field to drive away Hiuen-ts'e. The mission did not have an escort of more than a few dozens of cavalry; they could do nothing and all perished. The goods offered as tributes by the kings were all plundered. Wang Hiuen-ts'e escaped. He ran to the western frontier to *Tou-fan* (Tibet) and called the neighbouring countries to arms. Tibet supplied him with an army of 1,000 soldiers, Nepal gave him seven thousand cavalry. Hiuen-ts'e, dividing his army into several corps, advanced as far as the village of *Tch'a-pouo-ho-lo*[1], and after

1 The Sanskrit original of the name remains equally obscure as at the time of Pauthier and Julien. *Tch'a* is almost constantly equivalent to the long sounding cerebral '*da*'; *pouo*, to a labial; '*ho*', to '*va*', '*pa*' or '*ha*'; *lo* to a liquid. *Tch'a-pouo*, therefore, means the name of the country Ḍavāka, which is mentioned in the *praśasti* of Samudragupta (*Corpus*, III No. 1, I, 22), between 'Samataṭa' and Kāmrūpa in the same region within the border of Magadha. The two letters *ho-lo* are used in the word *Tan-ta-ho-lo*, for transcribing the component part *pāla* of the compound word *Daṇḍapāla*. The general note on India, which precedes the account in the *History of the T'ang*, indicates that the capital of the whole of Central India is named *Tch'a-pouo-ho-lo* which is situated on the bank of the river *Kia-pi-li*. One cannot take this to mean the Kāverī, which is phonetically equivalent to *Kia-pi-li*. Besides, Kapilī, (or Kapilā)—'brown'—is a very common name for rivers, and hence, cannot be located precisely. The most important Kapilī river is a tributary to the Brahmaputra, which flows in Assam, far from the frontier of Magadha. Ma-Toan-Lin identifies clearly the river Kia-pi-li with the Ganges: "The capital is situated on the river Heng-ho (Ganges) which is also named Kia-pi-li-ho" (note on India). The capital was not far from another river known as K'ien-to wei; here the original is restored with considerable accuracy; *Wei* means often '*vati*' (Prakrit '*wai*') as in *Che-wei* (Sāvatthī), *Fou-kie-la-wei* (Puṣkalāvatī), etc. *K'ien-to-wei* is equivalent to Gandavatī or Gaṇḍavatī, one of the possible forms for the name of the Gaṇḍakī (Cf. Gk. Kovdoxdns). It is, therefore, in the region between Pāṭaliputra, situated at the confluence of the Gaṇḍakī and the Ganges,

beseiging it for three days he captured the town. Three thousand men were killed and ten thousand persons were drowned in the river and died. O-lo-na-choen leaving the kingdom, fled and reassembled his troops and returned to offer another battle. Cheu-Jenn made him prisoner, killing about one thousand persons this time ; the others who were guarding the women of the royal household barred the crossing of the river K'ien-t'o-wei. Cheu-Jenn attacked them ; there was a great confusion. He imprisoned the wives and daughters of the king, and 12,000 persons and all the domesticated animals numbering some 30,000. He received the submission of 580 fortified towns. The king of Eastern India, Chi-kieou-mo (Śrī Kumāra) presented some 30,000 animals, oxen and horses for the army, and also bows, sabres and fringes. The kingdom of Kia-mou-lou (Kāmarūpa) offered to the emperor curios, a map of the country and wanted an image of Laotzeu as gift.[1] Hiuen-ts'e offered humbly to his emperor O-lo-na-choen as prisoner. The victory was proclaimed officially in the ancient imperial temple. Hiuen-ts'e was promoted to the rank of *tch' ao-san-ta-fou.*

---

and Nepal, whence issues the Gaṇḍaki, that one should look for the town of *Tch'a-pouo-ho-lo.* "The name of Kia-pi-li is again mentioned in the *History of the Song*, (Chap. 97, page 4a) as a kingdom of India. In the fifth year of the period *I-uen-kia* (428), the king of Kia-pi-li, *lue-ngai* ('Beloved moon'), sent an ambassador in 466. The '*Ancient History*' does not report the name of the capital and only mentions that "it was 70 *li* in circumference and that it was near the river *Chen-lien.*" It is quite probable that the *Chen-lien* was the Gaṇḍaki.

1 The king of Kāmarūpa was Kumāra, vassal of Śilāditya, who had sent pressing invitation to Hiouen-tsang to visit his kingdom (Memoirs, I, 254 and the subsequent pages). Kumāra appears to have practised the same religious dilettantism as his sovereign. Lao-tzeu had aroused his curiosity very strongly. Before sending a request through Wang Hiuen-ts'e to let him have a picture of the philosopher he had sent previously a similar request through Li-I-Piao. According to *Tsi-kou-kin-fou tao-loen-heng* (chap.2, end) compiled in 661 (Nanjio, 1471) in the year 21 of the period *Tcheng-koan* (647) the envoy Li-I-Piao on his return to China informed the emperor that the king T'oung-tzea ('son', *kumāra*) of Eastern India desired to obtain a Sanskrit translation of the book of Lao-tzeu. Hiouen-tsang was asked to get in touch with Taoist doctors for translating the work jointly ; but the attempt failed. The note on the kingdom of Kia-mou lou in the '*New History*' confused between the two requests : "When Wang Hiuen-t'se arrived, the king of that kingdom paid him tribute, including rare and precious objects and a map of his territory, and he begged to have, in return, a picture of Lao-tzeu and of Tao-te-king."

Ancient History of the T'ang Dynasty, Chap. 198

Before that incident (the return of Hiouen tsang) Wang Hiuen-ts'e who was *iou-wei-choai-fou-tch'ang cheu* was sent to India on a mission. All the kings of India sent through him tributes to the court. The king, who was ruling over central India, chi-lo-i-to, died ; the kingdom fell into anarchy. His ministeı No-fou-ti O-lo-no-choen captured the throne. He used in the campaign the troops of the Barbarians to attack Hiuen-ts'e. The mission did not have an escort of more than thirty cavalry men. They gave a fight to the barbarians but the party was not equal (to the enemy) ; when the arrows got exhausted, all were taken prisoners and the tributes given by the different kings were all plundered. Hiuen-ts'e alone escaped under the cover of night ; he fled to T'ou-fan (Tibet) which gave him 1,200 soldiers. Ni-po-lo gave him 7,000 cavalry. Hiuen-ts'e with the help of his assistant Tsiang Cheu-Jenn led the army of the two kingdoms, advanced as far as the capital of central India. The battle continued for three days, the loss was terrible. Three thousand persons were killed straight away and about 10,000 fell into water and were carried away. O-lo-Na-Choen fled from his capital. Cheu-Jenn pursued him, and made him captive along with 12,000 persons, men and women, and more than 30,000 animals, oxen and horses. India was thus conquered. Hiuen-ts'e brought to the capital (of China) his prisoner in the 22nd year (*Tcheng Koan*—648). He was promoted to the rank of *tch'ao-san-ta-fou.*

In the third chapter, p. 8, of the *Ancient History* we find that Wang Hiuen-ts'e returned along with O-lo-na-choen on *Keng-tzeu* day in the fifth month of the year 22 (648).

The Extracts of the Account

I. *Fa-iouen-tchou-li*, Chap. 4, p. 35, Col. 19, *Si-kouo-hing-tchoan* of Wang Hiuen-ts'e says : Wang, the ambassador in the year 4 of *Hien-k'ing* (659) arrived in the kingdom of *Po-li-che.*[1] In honour

1 The name of the country of *Po-li-che* corresponds to *Fo-li-che* of Hiouen-tsang, which is a translation of the Sanskrit name Vṛjjis. But it is not likely that the country of Vṛjjis had constituted a separate kingdom by the middle of the

of the Chinese, the king entertained him with a game, performed by five women. They were given three swords to enable them to pass the swords on from one to the other while playing; as the game proceeded the number of the swords increased to ten. Then they made rope tricks. They leaped in the air above the rope, put shoes on and then took them out. They freely handled three weapons during the play: dagger, shield, and spear. Then they played various tricks of all types, cutting the tongue, extracting the intestines etc. which cannot be properly described.

II. *Chap. 5, p. 48, Col. 11, Si-kouo-tchi* says: "In central India in the mountains, which stand south-east of the kingdom of *Cheu-po* (Campa), there is the cave of the *Siou-lo* (*Asuras*) in a rocky gorge. In the past there was a person who practised the religion going about in the mountains. He saw the great hall of the palace of *Siou-lo*, with flowers of such excellence that one would at once think himself to be in the palace of the gods. He also saw gardens, lakes, forests and fruits, in such a large number that they could not be counted. The *A-Sin-to* (*Asuras*) on seeing him said, 'Would you like to remain here for long or not?' He replied 'I would like to return to my abode.' The Asuras then saw that he would not stay there and gave him one peach and some food; then they told him 'It is necessary for you to leave this place quickly, as you will grow to such a dimension that the cave will be too small for your size.' And they asked him to run for getting out of the place. But, his body began to grow, and he assumed a colossal size. The head of the man just emerged, but the body became so big that it blocked the passage and he could not take it out completely. Since that time hundreds of years passed. The man had a big head of the size of three jars, but he could see, talk and tell the story of his adventure. The passers-by, taking pity on him, said, 'We are going to cut the rock to enable you to come out.

---

seventh century. Besides, the letter *po* used here represents by preference, the long-sounding labial; the letter *che* represents *Ja* or the combination: long-sounding dental+*ya*. The scene described here closely resembles that which the emperor of India held in honour of Wang Hiuen-ts'e; probably in both the passages the same games are meant.

What do all these mean ?' He replied, 'You will be too good to render me that service.' The people went to the king of the country and informed him about their intention. The ministers assembled and deliberated : 'He is not an ordinary man ; he has the strength to hold against 1,000 men ; if the rock is hewn to clear him out, he may put in his head some extraordinary ideas. How to resist him then ?' That is why the matter rested where it was. He was named, the giant with a big head.

The envoy of the T'ang, Wang Hiuen-ts'e went there three times ; he fingered the head by his hand and he talked with him, he understood him gradually more clearly and distinctly. Recently the country-people made a fire in the mountain. The head was burnt and charred, but the man, nevertheless. lived and did not die.

The sixty chapters of *Si-Kouo-tchi* were composed under the instruction of the government. The emperor had entrusted the work of preparing the maps to learned men of the highest rank (*hio-cheu*). The documents were assembled in Tchoung-t'ai. There are some 40 other books. Since the year 3 of *Lin-te* (666) the work was commenced, and it was completed towards the end of the summer of the year 1 of *K'ieu-feng* (666). Having seen Hiuen-ts'e myself I have collected all the information.

Then follows another legend, reported by Hiouen-tsang on another cave of the Asuras, situated in the kingdom *To-na-kia-tse-kia.*[1]

III. Chap. 7. p. *67. Col. 9.*

The *Hing-tchoan* of Wang Hiuen-ts'e says : "In the south-east of the kingdom of *Tou-fan* (Tibet) there is one gushing spring, which rises and springs up from a plain surface. The compressed water forms a fountain five to six *tch'eu* (feet) high ; it is hot. If one puts into the boiling water some meat, it is cooked forthwith. The vapour rises and condenses in the sky and forms a fog. An old Tibetan narrated that some ten years back the fountain rose to 100 feet high. In the beginning, the rim

---

1 Julien, *Mem.*, II, III, etc ; *cf.* there is still another similar legend, related by Hiouen-tsang, *Ibid.*, p. 14.

was gaping and it so happened that a person pursuing a deer went straight into it and was engulfed with his chariot and horses. Since that time the fountain does not rise so high. From time to time one can see the bones of a man thrown outside. If one hangs on water a woollen cloth, it gets changed at once and becomes disintegrated forthwith. One calls it "Kettle spring."

To the north-west of the fountain there is another thermal spring at a distance of sixty or seventy *li*; the temperature of the water does not remain constant. At times it is very active, and water of the spring, while rushing out, makes a noise of thunder. The smaller springs are generally tepid in most cases. And, now in *Tchen-tan* (*Cina-sthāna*, China) there are a number of tepid fountains in places. We may find out which of these are of the 'Kettle-spring' type. Hence in the *Vinaya of the four Sections* (*Dharmagupta-Vinaya*) the Buddha says 'To the north of the town of Rājagṛha, there is a hot spring. It comes from the centre of the underground world. Near its mouth the temperature of the water is in the boiling point; then flowing for some distance it gradually becomes cold, because other waters mingling with it lower its temperature'.—Extract from *Si-kouo-tchoan.*

IV. *Chap. 16, p. 15. Si-kou-hing-tchoan* of *Wang Hiuen-ts'e* says: In the Second year *Hien-king* (657) Wang and others were sent to the western kingdom by an imperial order, with a view to offering a *kasāya* to the Lord Buddha. They went lo *Ni-po-lo* (Nepal) towards south-west. On arriving at *P'ouo-lo-tou,* they proceeded to the east of the village towards the bottom of a depression. There was a small lake in flame. If one touches the water with a burning stick there appears all on a sudden a flame on the surface from the depths of water. If one wants to extinguish the fire by sprinkling water, it catches fire and burns. The Chinese envoy and his party placed a pot on the water and cooked their food. The envoy questioned the king of the country and the king replied: 'In olden times a box of gold used to appear when the water was struck with a cudgel; instruction was given to a person to take it out of water. But every time an attempt was made to lift it, it sank. Tradition says that it is the gold of the crown of *Mi-la-Pou-sa* (Maitreya

Bodhisattva), who is to come down to make the Law complete. The Nāga of fire protects and defends it, the fire of the lake was the fire of the Nāga of fire.

V. Chap. 29, p. 93b. Col. 10.

The author, summarising the account of travels of Hiouen-ts'ang, mentions the convent of the Ancient King in Kapiśa.[1] Now, in the beginning of the spring of the first year *Loung-so* (661) of the Great T'ang, the envoy Wang Hieun-ts'e returning from the western kingdoms gave presents officially.

VI. Chap. 29, p. 96.

During the period *Hien-king* (656-660) of the Great T'ang, by an imperial order Wang Hiuen-ts'e, the *wei-tch'ang cheu* (the chief of the guards and keeper of records) was entrusted with a mission. That is why he proceeded towards *In-tou* (India). He passed by the residence of *Tsing-ming* (pure glory=Vimalakīrtti). He measured it with his official staff (*hou*); it was exactly ten times its size (ten *hou*). It was why he named it 'Square tch'ang' (*tch'ang* is equivalent to a length of ten feet).[2]

---

1 Cf. Hiouen-tsang, *Mem.*, I, 53.

2 It is probable that the author of *Fa-iouen-tchou-lin* made here a confusion between the different travels of Wang Hiuen-ts'e. The Chinese envoy must have taken the measurement, which became well-known ever since, of the residence of Vimalakirtti at *Vaiśāli* before his third mission. *Cheu-kia-fang-tchi* of *Tao-siuen* dated, by its author, in the first year *Ioung-hoei* (650 B.C.) mentions this fact very precisely: "Recently, the envoy Wang Hiuen-ts'e has measured with his scale the site (of the residence of Vimalakirtti of Vaiśāli); he found exactly one *tchag* (=ten feet). Hence, he has named it 'Square tchang'. The passage of the *Fo-tsou-t'ong-ki* reported by Chavannes (*les Inscriptions Chinoises de Bodh-Gaya*, p. 28) is in accord with the findings of *Tao-siuen*: "In the 17th year *Tcheng Koan* (643 B.C.) *wei-wei-tch'eng Li-I-Piao*, and *hoang-choei-ling* Wang Hiuen-ts'e were sent to countries in the west by an imperial decree, and traversed through more than one hundred kingdoms. Arriving at the residence of Vimalakirtti, to the north-east of the town of Vaiśāli, Hiuen-ts'e measured it with his scale; both in length and in width it was ten *hou*; hence, *he* named it *fang-tchang*. Then he climbed up the mountain Gṛdhrakūṭa and there engraved an inscription to commemorate the glory and the virtue of the T'ang kings.""

Chap. 29, p. 97a, Col. 3

In the year 23 of the period *Tcheng-Koan* (648) there was an envoy who copied the foot print of the Lord Buddha.

VII. Chap. 29, p. 97b. Col. 2.

The *Hing-tchoan* of Wang Hiuen-ts'e says "In the western kingdom, the holy images are almost infinite in number. And with reference to the image under the tree of *Mo-ho-pou-t'i* (Mahābodhi) it says "Formerly the king of *Cheu-tzeu* (Ceylon) named *Chi-mi-kia-po-mo*, which means in Chinese 'merit cloud' (*Koung-te-iun*) (*Śrīmeghavarman*), the Indian king (*fan*) commissioned two *bhikṣus* to visit this monastery.[1] The elder of the two was named *Mo-ho-nan*, which means great name (Mahānāman). The other was named *Iou-po*, which means 'prophecy-give' (*Cheou-Ki*) (*Upa-*). The two *bhikṣus* paid homage to the Diamond throne (*Vajrāsana*) under the tree of Bodhi. The monastery did not offer them any shelter. The two *bhikṣus* returned to their country. The king questioned the *bhikṣus* "You had gone to pay your compliments to the sacred spots. What suspicious omen was found O *bhikṣus* ?' They replied 'In the large country of Jambudvīpa there is no place where we could live.' The king having heard them sent them with precious stones for offering to the king *San-meou-to-le-kin-to* (Samudragupta). And it is for that reason, uptil now, the *bhikṣus* of the kingdom of Ceylon are residing in that monastery.

As to the sacred image on the Diamond throne, at the time of sculpturing it, a stranger appeared and addressed the crown as follows : 'I understand that you want a clever artisan to make an image. I am a clever artisan and am capable of making it.' Tha crowd said, 'What things do you need for the execution of your work ?' He replied 'I want only some aromatics, water lamps, oil and wood at hand ; that will be enough.' Then, addressing the monks of the convent, he said 'I would like to have the door shut to enable me to model and sculpture and

1 The monastery built by Aśoka to the east of the tree of Bodhi, and later developed considerably. Cf. H. T., *Mem.*, I, 465.

none should open the door before the expiry of six months. It is not necessary to bring me food and drink.' Thus saying, the man entered and did not come out. But only four days before the expiry of these six months, the crowd began to discuss about this and could not decide anything.

Some said 'In the *stūpa* he is confined for so long and must have lost his life by now. Why should he stay continually for several months without opening the door and without letting us see him?' As they became suspicious, they opened the door of the temple and could not find the artist. The image was complete except that above the right heart some portions still remained to be done. And, a divine voice from the room said to the crowd 'I am Maitreya Bodhisattva.' The image is in a sitting posture in a east-west direction; its height is 1 *tch'ang*, 1 *tch'eu* and 5 *ts'uenn* (11½ feet), the shoulders are separated by 6 *tch'eu*, 2 *ts'uenn* (6.2 feet); the distance between the two knees is 8 *tch'eu*, 8 *ts'uenn* (8.8 feet). The Vajrāsana is 4 *tch'eu*, 3 *ts'uenn* high (4.3 feet); it is 2 *tch'ang*, 1 *tch'eu*, 5 *ts'uenn* (12.5 feet)[1] wide.

The king *A-iou* (Açoka) built the temple as a stūpa in the beginning, with a stone balcony. It was next rebuilt by two brahmins who were brothers: the elder was named *Wang-tchou* (king-master)(*Rājasvāmin*); the younger was *Fan-tchou* (*Brahmasvāmin*). The elder built up the temple 100 cubit high. The emperor[2] constructed the *vihāra*.[3]

Since Maitreya made the image, several attempts have been made to cast and reproduce it; but it is difficult to fix the holy sign and it has not yet been possible to obtain a reproduction. The envoy Wang (Hiuen-ts'e) put forward a demand to that effect to the assembly of monks. The personnel of the mission prayed solemnly and with great sincerety for practising the Law during a long succession of days, confessed their sins and declared their intentions to come back. Thus they succeeded

---

1 12.5 ft. should be 1 *tch'ang*, 2 *tch'eu* and 5 *ts'uenn*.

2 -'*ti*'-'emperor'. Can the letter *ti* be substitued by 'ti' 'the younger brother'?

3 Hiouen-tsang. *Mem.*, I, 465-66, relates the same story without giving the names of the two brothers. Cf. also Tārānātha, p. 64.

in obtaining a copy: it was almost similar to the original. And it was precisely for the image, the original of this *sūtra* was published. There have been only ten chapters till now. It should be propagated in the country. His artists, Soung Fa tche and others have succeeded by their talent to reproduce the whole face. After his return to the capital, monks and the laity became very eager to copy the model.

VIII. Chap. 29, p. 97b, Col. 16.

According to the Account (*tchoan*) of Wang Hiuen-ts'e "The chinese envoy, leading an imperial mission went to the kingdom of Magadha to the monastery of *Mo-ho-pou-ti* (*Mahābodhi*). He set up there a commemorative style. He had it erected to the west of the temple beneath Bodhi tree on the eleventh day of the second month in the year 19 of the period of *Tcheng-Koan* (645). He entrusted the writing to *T'ien-seu-men-ling cheu Wei Ts'ai.*"

IX. Chap. 29, p. 98. Col. 11.

According to the account (*tchoan*) of Wang Hiuen-ts'e issued in the third month of the year 17 of the period *Tcheng Koan* (643) of the great Tang, directing the dispatch of a mission to be led by *Tchao-san-ta-fou*, Li-I-piao, who was the *wei-wei*, in charge of temples and the chief protector of the army was to be assisted by the second-in-command Wang Hiuen-ts'e, a former chief administrator of Hoang-choei in the district of Ioung. The object of the mission was to accompany officially a Brahmin, a guest, who was returning to his country. In the twelfth month of that year they arrived in the kingdom of Magadha. They wandered over and visited the countries of Lord Buddha, and spent their time in contemplation of the existing holy vestiges. The spots containing the holy traces and the venerable transformations aroused their curiosity. On the 27th day of the first month of the year 19 (645) they arrived at the town on *Wang che* (Rājagṛha). They went up the summit of the hill *Ki-tche-kiu* (Gṛdhrakūṭa). They cast their contemplative looks; they looked on all sides endlessly. One thousand years after the Nirvāṇa the sacred footprints were just the same as they had been at the beginning. At every place where the Buddha had walked or stopped, was erected a commemorative *stūpa*.

Although my (Wang Hiuen-ts'e) abilities were quite a mediocre, I had the unexpected good fortune to see the venerable foot-prints. Sometimes sad, sometimes happy I could not control my feeling. It is why I have engraved an inscription on the mountain face so as to perpetuate an everlasting souvenir so that the emperor of the T'ang may have a splendour as durable as that of the sun and the moon, and the law of Buddha may be as extensive and as vast as this mountain and may obtain an equal strength.

X. Chap. 35, p. 37 ; Col. 14.

Si-iu-tchi, says : On one side of the forest there is a bench on which is placed a statue of Śākya Buddha, made of clay. He is leaning on the right side. The length of the body is 2 *tch'ang* 2 *tch-eu*, 4 *ts'uenn* (22.4 ft). A Kasāya of golden colour covers it. And even today it emits often a divine lustre. On the north-east of the town of *Wang-che* (Rājagṛha) is situated the mountain *Ki-tche-kiu* (Gṛdhra-Kūṭa) ; there one finds the petrified Kasāya of the Buddha. When the Buddha was alive, he placed his garment on the rock before going to take his bath in the lake. Once, a big vulture took his garment in his beak and flew away, the garment fell on the ground and was transformed into stone. The marks of the threads of warp and of the weft are seen even today. To the south of the rock, one can see Buddha imparting instructions to his disciple *Nan-to* on the cut of *Kasāya*. One sees there very often a marvellous glittering light. The envoy of the Great T'ang, Wang Hiuen-ts'e had gone there three times with his followers but never succeeded in seeing it.

XI. Chap. 38, p. 62 a, Col. 9.

Si-iu-tchi says : In the kingdom of *Kipin* (Kapiça) the doctrine of the Buddha is widespread. Within the capital there is a monastery, known as the Convent of the Han. Formerly, an envoy of the Han went to that country and there built a *Feou-t'ou* (*stūpa*) ; he built it on a pile of stones, 100 *tch'eu* (feet) high. The observance of religious cult differs there from all other rites. In the convent, there is a bone of the skull of the Buddha and also a hair of the Buddha, which is deep blue in colour and rolled up in the shape of a shell. They deposited it with seven precious things inside a gold box.

To the north-west of the capital there is a royal convent. A milk-tooth of Śakya Bodhisattva, the child lies there ; it is one inch long.

Proceeding further south-west, there stands a convent of the wife of the king. In that convent there is a copper *Feou-t'ou*, one hundred *tch'eu* (foot) high. In the *Feou-t'ou* there are relics. If one fasts there for six days, he can see a luminous light at night, the light circumambulates from the base to the dome ; and returns within at the day break.

XII. Chap. 38, p. 62a, Col. 12.

Si-iu-tchi says : At a distance of 100 *li* to the east of the capital of the king *Po-seu-ni* (Prasenajit) there is a grand *stūpa* on sea coast. Within the *stūpa*, there is a small *stūpa*, which is one *t'chang* and 2 *tch'eu* (12 feet high), and filled with precious things. Often at night it emits a light, which shines like a pile of fire. They say that five hundred years after the *Pan-nie-pan* (*Parinirvāṇa*) of the Buddha, *Long-Chou-Pou-sa* (Nāgārjuna Bodhisattva) entered into the ocean for converting the king of the dragons. The king of the dragons, holding that previous *stūpa*, offered it as a present to Nāgārjuna. Nāgārjuna having received it wanted to give it to that kingdom. The king gave orders to build up a large *stūpa* of a type which would hold it inside. From the olden times to the present epoch, persons desirous of some wish, place around the *stūpa* some perfumes and pay homage with a canopy of flowers. The canopy moves away from the ground, rises slowly by itself and stops just above the *stūpa* in the sky, and at day break it takes up some other form, and disappears without people knowing where it lies.[1]

Si-iu-tchi says : In the kingdom of *Po-lo-nai* (Benares) Nagārjuna Bodhisattva built seven hundred *stūpas*. As numerous other saints built innumerable *stūpas*, there are more than 1,000 *stūpas* cons-

1 This kind of wonder is also referred to in the account of Hiouen-tsan (*Mem.*, II, 89) on the *stūpa* of Puṣpagiri in the kingdom of *Ou-tcha* (Uḍa, Orissa).

tructed on the banks of the river *Chen-lien.*[1] Once in five years they convene a grand assembly of deliverance. (*Ou-tche ta-hoei* = "*mokṣa—grand assembly*").

XIII. Chap. 39, p. 69a, Col. 12.

Si-iu-tchi says : To the south-west of the kingdom of *Ou-tchang* (Udyāna) there is a mountain *Tan-te.*[2] In the mountain there

---

1 The river *Chen-lien* is mentioned in the ancient *History of T'angs*, on the banks of which stands the capital of Central India. The syllables *lien* and *chen* occur side by side; but in an inverse order in the transcription *Ni-lien-chen* which stands for the sanskrit word Nairañjanā, and *Hi-lien-chen* stands for Hiraṇyavati. The first of those two rivers flows near Gayā associated with the *Samyaksambodhi* of Śākyamuni ; the other river, which waters the territory of Kuśinagara, is the Gaṇḍaki. The identity of the two component parts *lien-chen* in both the names often gives rise to confusion between the two rivers. Hence, *I-tsie king in-i* of Hiuen-ing (chap. 3) writes *Ni-lien-chen* : it should be read as *Ni-lien-chen-na.* It is also called *Hi-lien-chen.* The translation is : *Ni*=no ; *lien-chen-na*=salve. Its means : The river without salve. The reversal of the sounds *chen* and *lien* might have been caused by the analogy of a number of expressions used in the Chinese Buddhism where *chen* (=*dhyāna*) figures foremost as a sort of adjective.

2 The mountain *Tan-te* is famous in the Buddhist tradition in the north because of the sojourn of the prince *Siu-ta-na*, one of the heroes of perfect benevolence at that place. *Siu-ta-na* corresponds exactly to Vessantara in the Pali literature. The name of the mountain is transcribed in Chinese in many ways. The ancient authors use the form *Tan-te* ; one comes accross this word in *Liou-tou-tsi king* (*Ṣaṭpāramitāsamnipāta ?*) translated by Kang Seng-hoei (222-280) (Edition Jap., VI, 5, p. 56) ; in *Siu-ta-na-king*, translated by Chang-kien (385-431) (Ed. Jap., VI, 5, p. 91 b) ; in the travel of Soung-iun, from which is borrowed this extract, as given in *Si-iu-tchi* (*Cf. Travels*, translation, Beal, p. 196). But the *Fan-fan-iu* of I-tsing, quoted in the dictionary Ekkō, gives as a correct transcription *Tan-to* which is interpreted as '*in*', 'shaded'.

I-tsie-king in-i of Hiuen-ing (note on the *Siu-ta-na-king*) mentions another transcription, *Tan to-lo-kia*, and translates it as *in* shade. Then, Hiouen-tsang, who visited the site, wrote *T'an-to-lo-kia* without translating the name, something unusual for him. Stanislas Julien thought himself justified in restituting the original Sanskrit, as Dantaloka, which has been accepted. But the interpretation of I-tsing and of Hiuen-ing showed the mistake of Julien ; moreover, the meaning *lo* given to the sign is not in accord with the usage ; *la*(*k*) invariably is used before *ka*, as for example in Āmalaka, Potalaka. Julien himself translated the same letter by *ra*(*k*) in Charaka the name of a convent in Kapiśa, adjacent, consequently, to the mountain *Tan-ta-lo-kia.* Finally, the

is a convent, inhabited by many monks. Every day an ass brings provisions, without being led by any body. It comes out of its own accord, leaves the provisions and returns. Impossible to know where it lives.

XIV. Chap. 39, p. 69a, Col. 12.

Si-iu-tchi says : In the year 5 of the period *Hieu-king* (660) of the Great T'ang, on the 27th day of the ninth month, Wang Hiuen-ts'e went to the monastery of Bodhi. The chief of the monastery (*seu-tchou, vihārasvāmin*), named Kiai loung (Śilanāga) held a grand assembly in honour of the Chinese mission. Every one placed offerings at the feet of the envoy, flowers, eight pieces of cloth and a pot of food ; then they requested the envoy to offer pearls of dragon etc. in the high place. Here is the complete list of the presents : real big pearls, eight boxes, an ivory *stūpa*, a precious *stūpa* with relics, four impressions

---

parallel transcription furnished by *I-tsie-king-in-i* attested the real pronunciation : *la*. But, all these do not facilitate the restitution of the original. The words 'shade' or 'shaded' do not call up equivalents in sanskrit of *Tan-to*, *Tan-to-lo-kia*. And, however, the description of the mountain, given by *Liou-tou-tsi-king*, tallies well with this interpretation : 'Arriving in the mountain *Tan-te*, the prince saw the mountain, the trees, the abundant vegetation, the running fountains, fine waters, savoury fruits.' The word *Tan-to-lo-kia* can be very well analysed in the two component parts : *tan-to* and the suffix *lo-kia*. What does *tan-to* mean ? The two letters used by Hiouen-tsang, and found again in *I-tsie-king in-i* of Hiouen-ing take the form *danta* (tooth) in sanskrit rendering. The name of 'good tooth', *Chen-ia* (Sanskrit *Sudanta*), given to the prince, appears to justify this interpretation ; but I-tsing and Hiuen-ing eliminate it entirely. Besides, the book of I-tsing quotes another word *Tan-te-heno-lo* which is corrected as *Tan-tcha-po-lo* and which is a transcription of Daṇḍa (pāla). Thus in common transcription *tan-te* should probably become Daṇḍa. The name of Daṇḍapiṅgalaka, which, according to the catalogues of Varāhamihira (*Bṛhat-Saṃhitā*, XIV, 27), was situated not far from Takṣaśilā and Puṣkalāvatī, has probably some connection with our mountain.—But the absence of this tradition to Hiouen-tsang, its similarity to the name *Cha-lo kia*, equally inexplicable, and the existence of Turkish populations, beyond any doubt, on the farthest frontier of India suggest another explanation. We are probably confronted with some Turkish name. In addition to that passage another extract from *Soung-iun* occurred through the medium of *Si-iu tchi* in *Fa-iuen-tchou-lin* (Ch. 38, p. 62 a). That is the description of the pagoda of Loriot (*Tsio li Feou-t'ou*) built by Kaniṣka in Gandhāra.

of the Buddha. On the first day of the tenth month, the *vihārasvāmin* and other monks escorted the envoy, who left. They accompanied him for a distance of 5 *li* towards the west and wept in silence and said, while parting, "Ah ! meeting is difficult, separation is easy, that is the universal law".

XV. Chap. 55, p. 47b, Col. 20.

During the reign of the dynasty of the Great T'angs, the emperor T'ai-tsoung (627-649) and the present emperor (Kao-tsoung) gave the charge of an official mission in the western countries to *tch'ao-San-ta-fou* Li-I-Piao, who was exercising the duties of *wei-wei*, assistant of the temple, and the chief protector of the army. They further appointed Wang Hiuen-ts'e as second-in-command, who was a former Chief administrator of Hoang-choei in the district of Ioung. The mission was given a guard of 22 men. And, on several other occasions others were sent. The former emperors also sent missions, and the intercourse had been frequent. Now, all of them visited the places where Bhagavat had in old times delivered the *sūtras*, and also saw the sacred vestiges.

XVI. Chap. 76, p. 66b, Col. 6.

In the 20th year *Tcheng-Koan* (646) of the great T'ang, five Brahmins from the western countries had gone to the capital city. They knew well music, magic and all types of tricks. They cut their tongue, extracted their intestines, ran on a rope, stopped all on a sudden on it and resumed running again. And in the period *Hien King* (656-661) Wang Hiuen-ts'e was sent to the five Indies. The emperor of the western country (Si-kouo-t'ien-wang) celebrated a treat in honour of the Chinese mission. There were men who leaped up in air, ran on a rope, walked over a rope with wooden shoes on. The men and women chased each other and ran while singing, and took a turn as easily as in a street. There was also a woman, who handled at the same time three weapons : a sword, a spear of cavalry, a post, and hurled them in air. She ran with clasped hands on the rope without falling. There were also others, who cut their tongue, rolled themselves, releasing and bending their body in an old fashion without showing any signs of fatigue. All types of tricks were also played, which cannot be properly described.

XVII. Chap. 91, p. 52a, Col. 15.

Hing-tchoan of Wang Hiuen-ts'e says : Here is the law of the kingdom of Magadha. If some one is guilty, he is not beaten by a rod, but recourse is taken to a wonderful weighing. The weighing is done as follows : One gets hold of certain articles which form exactly the counter-weight of the man. The guilty is placed on one of the scales of the balance and the articles on the other. When both the scales are in equilibrium, a tablet (*fou*) is prepared and the counter-weight is exactly made out with the help of this object. Then, on one side the tablet is attached to the back of the neck of the guilty person, and on the other are added the articles which were previously weighed against the person. If the person is innocent, the weighing articles would be heavier. If he is guilty, those articles would be lighter. The nature of punishment corresponds to the difference in weight ; the eyes may be severed, the wrist may be cut or fingers or feet may be removed. They also note the gravity of the offence for giving punishment. If the offence is slight, as for example in the case of non-payment of debt, the two legs are joined together with a chain by way of punishment.[1]

---

1 The method of the weighing as used in Magadha, as reported by Wang Hiuen-ts'e, differs by an important detail, firstly, from the description given by his contemporary Chinese envoy and Hiouen-tsang (*Mem.* I, 84) and, secondly, from that given by the Indian authorities, Yāgñavalkya, Viṣṇu, Nārada and Pitāmaha. The Characteristic of the ordeal, according to our text, is the intervention, in the weighing, of a tablet in which the accusations brought against the person are inscribed. Viṣṇu, Yāgñavalkya, and Hiouen-tsang ignore completely the tablet. Pitāmaha (2, 26, 28) and Nārada (1, 276, 295) —(I borrow those references from J. Jolly, *Rechlund Sille*, 145, but the translation of Nārada by the same author shows nothing to correspond to it),—have mentioned "Round the head of the accused a piece of paper is attached, in which the accusations brought against him are written, and also a form of adjuration" (Stenzler, *Z.D.M.G.*, IX, 667). But those two authors considered that that method was adopted only when the first weighing did not give any result. The addition of a written papei is destined to disturb an equilibrium already difficult ; but the disturbance would be more by its magieal force

XVIII. Chap. 98, p. 92a, Col. 14.

Hing-tchoan of Wang Hiuen-ts'e says, The chief of the monastery (*seu-tchou, vihārasvāmin*) of Bodhi in the kingdom of Magadha, master of law (*ta-mo-che, dharmācārya*) questioned the envoy of the Chinese emperor. Being informed that the law of the Buddha prevails in China, the master of the law said "The law of the Buddha now prevails in the four cardinal points. Formerly, the king, Kia-Kie (Karka, Kṛkin) saw in a dream that the waters of the ocean were agitating in the middle, and were calm on the four coasts. Kāçyapa Buddha, who was requested to explain the dream, told him, 'Later on, the law of the Buddha Śākyamuni will disappear from Central India, that is why the water is agitating in the middle. It will propagate in the four borders, that is why the water is calm on the coasts'.[1]

---

than by its real weight, since one overlooks to note the deficiency. In Magadha, on the other hand, if the statement of Wang Hiuen-t'se is true, the tablet was used from the first and the weight was quite considerable so that one could allow the deficiency apart. The agreement, though incomplete, between our text and that of Nārada, appears to support the opinion which attributes to that law code a late date.

1 The words addressed to Wang Hiuen-t'se by the chief of the convent at *Mahābodhi* lends further confusion to the matter relating to the Dreams of Kṛkin, which was already found difficult to interpret. Serge d'Oldenbourg (*J.R.A.S*, 1893, 509-516) and Tsuru Matsu Tokiwai (*Studien Zum Sumāgadhāvadāna*, 1898 pp. 12-15), have pointed out and compared the verious texts of the Ten Dreams, equally popular in both the sections of the Buddhist Church and also found in the Persian literature. The particular dream, which has been recalled here, was totally left out in the sanskrit editions (*Sumāgadhāvadāna*, *Abhidharmakoṣa* and Commentaries). It is the ninth in Pali edition (Jātaka 77), and found in four Chinese versions. But, invariably, all the texts, where it appears, subtitute, without fail, the king Prasenajit for the king Kṛkin, and, necessarily the Buddha Śākyamuni for the Buddha Kāśyapa. We know, henceforth, through the writing of Wang Hiuen-t'se that there existed in the seventh century in Central India a text on Ten Dreams in which occurred the dreams as noted in the texts of Chinese-Pali, and of the great men as noted in the Sanskrit text; the book which contained these combined texts was held canonical in the convent of *Mahābodhi*. Besides, the blending of the two texts into one in the convent can be very well explained, because of the fact that the convent was frequented by Singhalese religious persons, who followed the Pali tradition, but was built in the centre of Sanskrit orthodoxy.

XIX. Chap. 100, p. 106, Col. 6.

According to *Si-iu-hing-tchoan* of Wang Hiuen-ts'e, in the kingdom of Magadha, at the monastery of the Bodhi, the venerable monk (*ta-te, bhadanta*) *Che-na-k'ia-sien-to,* has calculated and published the following based on the Sūtras: Śakya Bodhisattva left the village at night when he was nineteen years four months and fifteen days old; at the age of thirty he perfected the way; at the age of seventy-nine he entered in the Nirvāṇa. Calculating up to the present year, the year 2 of Hien-heng (671) appears to have occurred 1395 years ago.

(Say 724 B.C. for the date of the *Nirvāṇa.* But in the same book, Chap. 29. 96a, Col. 11, we find "In the year 3 *Loung-so* (663) the people say that 1200 years elapsed since the *Nirvāṇa* (say 537 B.C.) It is based on an inscription found on a stone-column at the monastery of Bodhi. According to others, 1300 years, 1500, and more than 900, but without completing a millenium cf. Hiouen-tsang, *Mem.*, I, 335)

XX. Chap. 100, p. 102a, Col. 1.

Tchoung-T'ien-tchou-hing-ki. 10 books, I volume. Author: tch'ao-san-ta-fou Wang Hiuen-ts'e. *Si-iu-tchi* 60 books. Maps and sketches, 40 books. The whole forming two volumes and 100 books in total. Compiled under the order of the emperor by one hundred officials in the year 3 *Lin-te* (666).

The Inscription of Wang Hiuen-ts'e Translated by Chavannes

Chavannes, who had already published a remarkable work on the Chinese inscriptions at Bodh Gayā (*Revue de l'Historie des Religions*, 1896, No. 1), is now pleased to undertake the translation of the inscriptions engraved by Li-I-Piao and Wang Hiuen-ts'e on the Gṛdhrakūṭa and at Mahābodhi. None of the original slabs has yet been recovered. Thanks to Grierson, I have climbed up the slopes of Gṛdhrakūṭa in the hope of finding the stone slabs which bore the inscriptions of the Chinese envoys. The bushy vegetation, which spread over all the place and made it impossible for one to ascend the hill, was primarily responsible for my failure. I am certain that systematic research in the sacred mountain will result in the discovery of important finds, the cirque of Rājagṛha, abandoned to nature for the last so many centuries, contains hidden treasures of an ancient historical period.

Inscription made on the Gṛdhrakūṭa on the 28th February, 645 A.D., by the Chinese mission of which Wang Hiuen-ts'e was a member (*Fa yuen tchou lin, chap. XXIX, p. 98b, Col. 16*) :

FIRST STANZA

The Great T'angs appear with the mark tchen ;[1] their opportune politics has
the flight of a dragon :
Their glory occupies[2] throughout
the length and breadth of the earth ;[3]—
Their charity reaches to the four
cardinal points as far as the barbarians.
Their transforming act rises
higher than three and five ;[4]
Their virtue surpasses that
of (Hien)-Yuen and (Fou)-hi.[5]
Fairly high up they suspend the Jade Mirror ;[6]—
with robes hanging and clasped hands
they do not have to act.[7]

---

1 *Cf.* I King, Chap. XVII, p. 7, (Legge, S.*B.E.*, Vol. XVI, p. 425) : "The Emperor appeared with the sign of tchen." (The trigram *tchen* symbolises the East).

2. *Cf.* Preface of *chou king* (Legge, *C.C.*, Vol. III, p. 1) : "His glory filled up the empire."

3 Nowhere in the world there could be found one who was not a subject of the king, as indicated by Legge.

4 The expression refers to the constellations, Scorpion and Hydre, which consist of three and five stars respectively. According to other explanations, the numbers 3 and 5 relate to diverse astronomical assemblages ; *Cf. Sema Ts'ien*, French translation, Vol. III, p. 410, line 27. Whatever explanation one may adopt, the wordings of the inscription signify that the transmutations operated by the T'angs rise higher than the stars.

5 *Fou-hi* and *Hien-yuen* (or *Hoang-ti*) are two mythical kings of the Chinese antiquity.

6 Symbol of a match-less lustre.

7 Without interference and only by their power the empire was found to have

SECOND STANZA

The Taoists prescribed to follow the nature ;
the men of letters were honoured
in conformity with the time ;
They secured repose for the superiors[1]
and practised the rites ;—
They modified the habits and regulated them.
(But), having taken birth
in the middle of the earth,[2]—
they were not lumped together
in sheets of paper and did not
spread in remoter places.[3]
(On the contrary) when the Buddhist religion
came in the country—
it spread without any limit.

THIRD STANZA

The divine power is predominant ;[4]
the opportune transmutation is limitless ;
Sometimes they spring from the earth ;
sometimes they fall from the high heaven
(sometimes they are god-sent).
During the ten millions of days and
months ; in the three thousands of
tens of thousands (of the Universe).

---

been governed well. The falling robes and the clasped hands imply immobility. *Cf. Chou king*, Chap. *Ou tch'eng* (Legge, *C.C.* Vol. III, p. 316) : "He let his robes fall and clasped his hands and the empire was well governed."

1 Cf. *Liki*, chap. *king Kie* (Legge, *S.B.E.*, Vol. XXVII, p. 258) "For securing peace for the superiors and for governing the people well, there is nothing as good as the rites." The same text is found in *Hiao king* (Legge, *S.B.E.*, Vol. III, p. 482).

2 Here this expression refers to China.

3 In other words, Taoism and Confucianism are purely Chinese doctrines and do not pretend to have the universality of Buddhism.

4 This expression implies the idea of sovereignty ; *cf.* Maheśvara named "the great sovereign."

FOURTH STANZA

Vast is the mountain ;[1]—the
extraordinary sceneries repeat ;
Higher up, it goes as far as
the rarefied clouds ;—lower down,
it reaches the dashing waves.
In all the places where it has
descended it plays the rôle of holy
supernatural power,—in all the places
traversed by the perfect sage,
are conserved the sacred traces ;
On the menacing peaks,—
the foot-prints are kept in the inmost
recess of the escarpments.

FIFTH STANZA

The uneven heights[2] are the precipitous peaks ;—
the numerous folds are the high galleries ;[3]
Resonant like jade is the precious bell ;—
the exceptional perfumes are sweet ;
Having meditated the sacred
foot-prints on the beautiful mountain,—
I engraved a veridical inscription
on the majestic peak,
To give free scope to the excellent transmutation
operated by the Great T'angs—
and for equalising in eternity
the Heaven and the Earth.

---

1 The Gṛdhrakūṭa.

2 This expression in *Che-king* (*Kouo Fong*, 1st Book ; Legge, *C. C.*, Vol. IV, p. 1) refers to the plants which thrive in the uneven heights.

3 The author of the inscription compares the counterparts of Gṛdhrakūṭa with longitudinal galleries which occur on both sides of a palace.

II

Inscription erected at the foot of the Bodhidruma on the 14th March, 645 A.D.

(Fa Yuen tchou lin, Chap. XXIX, p. 97, Col. 18)

In former times, when the (dynasties) Hans and Weis reigned[1] and governed, they exhausted their arms in waging war. The soldiers who took part in the campaign numbered one hundred thousand; their daily expenses amounted to one thousand monetary units.[2]

Then again they would not be checked as far as north of *T'ien-yen*[3] and conferred the investiture to the *Pounai*[4] in the east. The great (dynasty) T'angs obtained their captures from the six directions of space.[5] They surpassed hundred other kings[6] in wisdom. Wherever their shining force is applied under the vast sky, all men become submissive.

Hence in the different kingdoms of India religious persons and the laity have attached themselves to the dynasty with sincerity; the emperor had compassion for their loyal wishes;

---

1 The dynasties of Han and Wei cover the period 206 B. C.—265 A.D.

2 The book entitled 'The Military Art' writes "when ten thousand soldiers are employed in a campaign, the expenditure per day amounts to one thousand monetary units".

3 *T'ien-yen* is the name of a mountain in the country of the *Hiong-nous*: here this expression refers to the *Hiong-nous* themselves. The mountain *T'ien-yen* is mentioned, with a slight variation of orthography, in the biography of *Houo K'iu-p'ing* (*Ts'ien Han Chou*, Chap. LV. p. 5): "He arrived then near the mountain *T'ien-yen* and the town of *Tchao-sin*; he seized the grains stored by the *Hiong-nous* for feeding the army.

4 In the quotations furnished by *P'ei wen yun fou*, the term *Pou-nai* does not refer to the name of a country. However, as the term here corresponds to the term *T'ien-yen* of the preceding phrase, it may be taken to mean the people of some country; it signifies probably "the unbearables" and could then be the surname less flattering than the eastern barbarians. The first part of the inscriptions can be interpreted as follows: The kings of the dynasties of *Han* and *Wei*, in spite of frequent wars, hardly succeeded in imposing their supremacy over Mongolia and Korea. How more glorious is the politics of the T'angs, whose prestige was known througout the world, and particularly in India.

5 The four cardinal points and up and down.

6 That is to say he is superior to all the kings who ever ruled.

far away he was absorbed in the care of holy persons; that is why, under his order, the ambassador *Li-I-Piao* who had the rank of *tch'ao-san-ta-fou*[1], who exercised the rôle of the assistant in the department of *wei-wei*[2] and who had the title of the chief protector of the army,—the vice-ambassador Wang Hiuen-ts'e who had been previously deputy-chief of the sub-division of *Hoang-choei*, in the district of Yong[3],—and their assistants, in all twentytwo persons, travelled over the kingdoms to cheer up the people. They arrived then on the site of the temple of *Mahābodhi*, to the diamond throne, which was at the foot of the tree of the Bodhi; it is there that thousand Buddhas of the *Kalpas* of the sages have attained salvation; the majestic ornaments, the distinctive primary and secondary marks[4] are complete as on the true face.[5]

The supernatural *stūpas* and the genuine spots form an art which shine to the end of the regions beyond the heaven[6], it is that which has remained unseen yet, even in the distant generations, and has not yet been described in the memories of historians. Far away, the emperor has stirred his majestic

---

1 *Tch'ao-san-ta fou* is an honorary title given to civil mandarins; the title, *Li tai tche koan piao* is identified with the modern titles of *Fong-tcheng ta fou* and *fong-tche-ta-fou* which occupy the fifth rank in an hierarchy of the ninth degree (*cf.* Mayers, *The Chinese Government*, p. 64)

2 The *wei wei* was the commander of the imperial bodyguard.

3 This sub-division of *Hoang-choei* has not been mentioned in the dictionary of the historical geography of *Li-Tchao-lo*, but there has been mentioned the district of Yong, which must have been close to the sub-division of that name in the secondary district of Lieou in the province of *Koang-si*.

4 The body-marks distinguish the Buddha from other men. One finds in an article by de Harlez (*Toung poo*, Vol. VII, pp. 364-372) the list of 32 distinctive primary and 80 distinctive secondary marks.

5 It refers here to the statue of the Buddha, which is kept in the temple of *Mahābodhi*; it was the work of a person, who was taken to be an incarnation of Maitreya Bodhisattva *Cf. Hiouen-tsang*, I, p. 142 and II, p. 467; Foucher, *L'art bouddhique dans l'Inde* (*Revue de l'Histoire des religions*, XXX, pp. 26-30).

6 This metaphor is used to indicate something as vast as one can conceive of. *Cf.* A text in *Tch'ang Heng* cited in *P'ei wen yun fou*: "That grandeur is so vast that it has no limit, and now it is certain that it extends as far as the farthest end of regions lying beyond the heaven".

authority and illuminated[1] the tree of the Bodhi in a brilliant manner. Consequently he instructed his ambassadors, when they would reach the place, to meditate it with respect; that perfect deed, which does not belong to this world, is divine, and will not fall into oblivion. How can one express it in songs but fail to transmit it on metal or stone? They have therefore made this inscription in rhyme.

FIRST STANZA

When the great T'angs[2] rule, the opportune
politics is lasting and flourishing;
They operate the transmutation in six directions
of space; they exercise their supernatural
power over eight barbarian countries;
India has prostrated her head;—religious
persons and the laity came to acknowledge
their sovereign.[3] It is, therefore (the
T'angs) distinguished ambassadors were sent
to contemplate the area of the wisdom (*bodhimaṇḍa*)

SECOND STANZA

On the diamond throne (*Vajrāsana*)—
the thousand Buddhas are held in turns.
The distinctive primary and secondary marks
On the venerable face—are the models
prepared by Maitreya.

---

1 This expression occurs in a song which *T'chou chou ki nien* attributes to the emperor Choen (*Cf.* Legge, *Chou king*, prol., p. 115): "The brightness of the sun and the moon renew from morning to morning."

2 *Cf. Ts'ien Han chou*, chap. LIV. p. 2 "His supernatural influence incites fear of the neighbouring kingdoms". The commentator *Li Ki* explains the word *leng* saying: "The word *leng* connotes the influence of a divine and supernatural influence."

3 *Cf. Chou king*, chap. *Ta Yu Mo* (Legge, *C. C.*, Vol. VIII, p. 54)—"The barbarians from four cardinal points come to acknowledge their sovereign."

The supernatural wall[1] is beautiful and admirable ;—
the tree of intelligence is exuberant ;[2]
How does this divine force level up the people ?[3]

The Inscription of Mahānāman at Mahābodhi

Hiouen-tsang gives a vague account of the origin of the convent of the *Sthaviras* (elders) at *Mahābodhi* : The younger brother of a king of Ceylon, left on a pilgrimage to holy places, and received there bad reception ; on returning to his home island he urged his elder brother to construct with the consent of the king of India a monastery near *Bodhidruma*, for lodging the Sinhalese religious persons (I, 487 and sub.). Wang Hiuen-ts'e is more precise ; he gives the names, and those names imply a date. The king of Ceylon, Śrī Meghavarman[4] (or rather *Meghavarṇa* ; the Chinese, ignorant of the niceties of the Sanskrit language confused the word *varṇa* with *varman*, common suffix of royal names), and the king of India, Samudragupta, are already known to historians. As regards other less important personages, Mahānāman and Upa, one of them is named in two inscriptions found on the same site of Mahābodhi, and made known by Fleet (*Ind. Antiq.*, XV 356 and 359 ; *Corpus*, III, 274 and 278). The one, very short, commemorates the erection of a statue by Mahānāma (*Mahānāmasya*), the *Sthavira* (elder) inhabitant of Āmaradvīpa ; the other, pretty long, celebrates the construction of a religious edifice by Mahānāman, and associates with his

---

1 *Cf. Hiuen-tsang*, translation, Julien II, p. 139 : "This tree (the *Bodhidruma*) is protected by brick walls, very high and massive, which are very long from east to west and narrow appreciably from south to north."

2 The dictionary of *K'ang-hi* gives the following definition : "The word *fou-chou* means the spreading branches and leaves." *Cf. T'sien Han Chou*, chap. LXIII, p. 4. "When the branches and leaves (of the imperial family) are thriving, the members of other families cannot interfere there."

3 That is to say : how does the divine force, which passes through *kalpas* without fail, make it equal ?

4 Pali *Sirimeghavaṇṇa*, A. D. 362-409. He was the son of Mahāsena. He is said to have constructed eighteen *vihāras* (monasteries) *Cūḷavaṃsa* (PTS), XXXVII, 53ff.—B. C. L.

pious work the lineage of his spiritual masters; they are in an ascending time-scale: Upasena, Mahānāman, Rāhula, Bhava. The Chinese transcribes and translates correctly the first name: *Mo-ho-nan* ('great name'). The companion of Mahānāman is more puzzling. *U-po* is an abbreviated form, which can also be represented by the Sanskrit word *Upaka*, all the names commencing with the prefix *Upa*. The alternation of the names of *Mahānāman* and of *Upasena*, in the spiritual genealogy of the Sinhalese monks, presumably refers here to an *Upasena*. But the Chinese interpretation which accompanies the transcription does not agree with that restoration: the Sanskrit-Buddhist term *Vyākaraṇa*[1] i.e. 'prophecy', is invariably translated as *Cheou-ki* i.e. 'To make announcement'. I do not know of any Upasena who had been the subject of a *vyākaraṇa*, of a prophecy owed to the Buddha. The only persons of that name that I came across in the canonical texts are Upasena, the nephew of the three Kāśyapas[2], and Upasena Vaṅgantaputta.[3] The latter gained his notoriety for a blunder; he had granted an irregular ordination, and received a blame from the Buddhist public. The other, converted to the religious faith, immediately after his three uncles, remained as a tame figure, although his name appears in the title of two chapters of the life of the Buddha (*Fo-pen-hing-tsi-king*, Chaps. 42 & 43: *U-po-sien-na-p'in* = Upasenavarga). Moreover, the *Mahāvastu* disagreeing with all the tradition, introduced a Upasena in place of Aśvajit during the conversion of Sāriputra and Maudgalyāyana (III, 60 ff). It is curious to note that Eitel, in his *Handbook of Chinese Buddhism*, translates the Sanskrit word 'Upasena' by the Chinese word *Ngo-pi* and adds 'a military title like *Aśvajit*'. In fact *Ngo-pi* is a regular transcription of the name Aśvajit and is quoted as such in *Fan-i-ming-i-tsi* (I, chap. 7), whereas Upasena is translated by *Tsoei-chang-tcheng-tsiang*, i.e. chief commander (*ibid.* chap. 9).

---

1 It is generally used in the sense of exposition or explanation or declaration. It is rarely used as forecast or prophecy—B. C. Law.

2 Uruvela-Kassapa (*Theragāthā*, PTS., vs. 375-380), Nadi-Kassapa (*Theragāthā*, vs. 340-44) and Gayā-Kassapa (*Theragāthā* vs. 345-49) were the three Kassapas or Kāśyapas (*Vinaya*, I, 24ff).—B. C. L.

3 *Theragāthā* (PTS) vs. 577-86.—B. C. L.

What is the source of Eitel's information? I could not find out the source, but the confusion between those two words appears to have arisen during the substitution effected by the *Mahāvastu.*[1] If Upasena is a duplicate of Aśvajit, the pair Mahānāman-Upasena (=Mahānāman—Aśvajit) recall two of the five *bhikṣus*, who became the first listeners of the Buddha. But the problem as it appears, has not yet been solved correctly in the absence of enough data.

Mahānāman[2], in the shorter of the two inscriptions, takes the title of *sthavira* (elder). Fleet derives from the simple word some conclusions on the age of Mahānāman and the date of his ordination. It appears to me that the term *sthavira* means here a school to which Mahānāman belonged with pride. At the time of Hiouen-tsang the religious persons of the Sthavira school were still in possession of a monastery (I, 488). The evidence of Wang Hiuen-ts'e enables us to put forward a new solution on an important point. The larger inscription of Mahānāman is dated the year 269. But of what era? The learned editor of *Corpus* is definite about this and says: "It is probable that the (second) Mahānāman, mentioned in the inscription, is identical with the person of the same name, who has composed the earliest part of the *Mahāvaṃsa.* Now, on the one hand, no body can doubt that the date of the present inscription must belong to the Gupta period, which means 588 or 589 A.D. On the other hand, Turnour, with the help of Singhalese annals, concluded that it was 459-477 A.D., corresponding to the period of the reign of Dhātusena[3], nephew of Mahānāman; and it was during his reign that Mahānāman prepared that historic compilation. The date of the present inscription is fixed then, if the proposed identification is admitted; however defective the details of Singhalese annals may be, and however erroneous the starting point for that interpretation may be, and which may now require considerable rectification". The dilemma, as it occurs very often, has an evasion; and it was that which enables one to put forward

1 I, 138; III, 431—B. C. Law.

2 409-31 A. D. During his reign Buddhaghosa came to Ceylon—B. C. Law.

3 Cf. *Cūḷavaṃsa*, xxxviii, 14 ff, 30 ff. Some have fixed his date at 460—78 A.D.—B. C. Law.

a third solution. The mention of Samudragupta and of Śrī Meghavarṇa as the contemporaries of Mahānāman, excludes, henceforth, the possibility of lowering the date to 269 in the Gupta period. The *Mahāvaṃsa*, in fact, noted that Kitti Siri Meghavaṇṇa[1] reigned from 304 to 332 A.D., and if the Singhalese Chronology cannot be taken too seriously, it hardly leaves, at any rate, any scope, too much restricted to undergo corrections. To solve the preliminary questions raised by Fleet, I have consulted the notes on Ceylon, as embodied in the Chinese Annals, and have included the translation of that memoir. The accuracy of the Singhalese Annals comes out clearly by that comparison.

The king Samudragupta certainly reigned, like Śrī Meghavarṇa, in the fourth century; but the exact period of his reign cannot be determined accurately. He is (if one leaves aside. as is done regularly in the epigraphic formulary, the enigmatic Kāca) the second king of the Gupta dynasty, founded in the year 319 A.D. The eulogy of Samudragupta, composed by Harisena, and engraved on the pillar at Allahabad, does not give any date; to find out a date, one has to come down to the reign of the son af Samudragupta, Candragupta II, in the beginning of the fifth century (82 *samvat* = 401 A.D.; *Corpus* No. 21). Samudragupta reigned any time in between the two years (319-401), without of course covering the whole of the period. Vincent Smith, who has contributed so much to throw light on the history of the Guptas, puts approximately the reign of Samudragupta between 345 and 380 A.D.[2] The relation of Samudragupta with Ceylon is noted in the panegyric at Allahabad; the Saiṃhalas there figure in the list of subject peoples, next to the group Daivaputra-Ṣāhi-Ṣāhānuṣāhi-Śaka-Muruṇḍa.[3] I have already had occasion to point out, in reference to the same group, about the accuracy of the official panegyrist. I would like to establish that the peoples, united thus in a single compound-name, were drawn together, in reality, by an original kinship.[4] As to Ceylon, Vincent Smith had first

1 Vide *Cūḷavaṃsa*. chs. 41 & 73—B. C. Law.

2 *J. R. A. S.*, 1897, p. 909.

3 Vide B. C. Law, *Tribes in Ancient India*, ch. XXII.

4 *Memoir of Harlez*, p. 183.

considered the reference as a 'simple matter of rhetoric'; but a fresh examination of the facts changed his opinion, and he "does not doubt any longer that an ambassador from Ceylon really visited the court of Samudragupta." Wang Hiuen-ts'e confirms and perfects Harişeņa, and Hiuen-tsang, in his turn, agrees to this when he says "The king of Ceylon offered to the king of India the treasures of his kingdom. When the king (India) had received the tribute......". (I, 489-490). One would like to read the commentary of the Sanskrit panegyric.

It can no longer be the question of restoring the date of the inscription of Mahānāman to the Gupta period; the Kalacuri period, which Fleet himself, hesitatingly proposes furthermore, in the Index of *Corpus*, would not be accepted any longer. The year 518 A.D. is impossible, equally impossible is the year 588. The hypothesis, which, from now on, seems to be the most plausible, is the consideration of the year 269, as expressed in the Śaka period; it corresponds then to 347 A.D. It falls, therefore, in the reign of Samudragupta; but it is, truly, fifteen years behind the date of Mahānāman, following the chronology of the *Mahāvaṃsa*. This point hardly discredits the important Annals, which refer to a remoter date,—an error, though slight. The establishment of the monastery at Mahābodhi tallies well, among others, with the character of Śrī Meghavarṇa[1], as represented in the *Mahāvaṃsa* of high piety, in love with processions and religious pomps, passionately devoted to Mahendra, the son of Aśoka and the apostle of Ceylon. The holy land of Magadha was the father-land of Mahendra; for this, hc gained, undoubtedly, an additional sanctity in the eyes of the Singhalese king. The travel of Mahānāman and the construction of the convent are probably in direct relation with the favourite saint of Śrī Meghavarṇa.

It is interesting to observe, in this connection, what political importance could be attached to the possession of the holy spots. The accounts of Chinese pilgrims indicate that every national Church aspired to own its particular convent near the sanctified sites, and especially near *Mahābodhi*. The Turks even competed

1 King of Ceylon (362—409 A.D.)—vide *Cūḷavaṃsa* chap. xxxvii. 53ff.—B. C. L.

in zeal with the Hindus.[1] The ruler of the country, if he considered himself strong enough, would not grant a concession of land without taking, in exchange, an appreciable amount of profit. Among the tributes of subjection, which Samudragupta received with pride, more than one were of the same type as the tribute paid by Śrī Meghavarṇa; more than one were meant as payment for the site, or for the purchase of land, for constructing a national monastery.

Before leaving Mahānāman, I would like to emphasise on two facts, which deserve consideration. Firstly, the use of Sanskrit by a monk of the school of Sthavira, towards the middle of the fourth century, though Buddhaghosa had written important works in Pali earlier. The victory of Sanskrit over the Prakrits as an epigraphic language was complete; the dialect of the Singhalese Church, whatever it was at that time, was not considered sufficiently dignified so as to be engraved on stone. The author of the inscription, whoever he was, either Mahānāman by name, or one of the Magadhan fellow members used Sanskrit with ease and skill; his compositions were well arranged, and successfully balanced; he grouped there frequently three or four words, and sometimes as many as five. The component parts of the phrase were balanced with a remarkable symmetry. He also knew how to change successfully the metres; out of eight stanzas, three were in *śragdharā*, two in *āryā*, two in *śārdūlavikrīḍita*, and one in *śloka*. The entire composition, taken together, occupies an intermediate place between the inscription of Rudradāman at Girnar, and that of Samudragupta at Allahabad, which mark so clearly two stages in the epigraphic literature.[2]

Another inscription, characterised by its commonplace brevity, when compared with that learned inscription, presents a striking contrast. The genitive *Mahānāmasya*, in front of the regular nominative *Mahānāma*, used in the first text, is sufficient to reveal the existence of an author more familiar with Prakrit than with Sanskrit. Whether Mahānāman was personally responsible for this breach of syntax or whether the choice of

1 Cf. p. ex. I-tsing, tran. Chavannes, p. 80.

2 Cf Buhler, *Die indischen Inschriften und das Alter der indischen Kunstpoesie*, *Wien*, 1890.

his epigraphist has been less happy this time, it appears clearly that Sanskrit again relapsed into Prakritism. There was nothing unexpected in a phenomenon like this, in the beginning of the fourth century.

The second point, which needs emphasis, is the use of the era 78 A.D. Samudragupta, in the beginning of his conquests did not overthrow the authority of the Śākyas and with it counted the Kṣatrapas, maintained by a long succession of kings, spreading out by the conquest, and prevailing till the farthest end of the empire, which sprang up from the Guptas. A little later, after the travel of Mahānāman, the new dynasty imposed successfully on the Hindu vassals the era of 319, which commemorated its foundation, and the era of the Śakas disappeared from the official records till again taken up much later. Mahānāman is dated 269; the coins of the latter known Kṣatrapas, and probably the last Kṣatrapa, Rudrasiṃha, bears the date 310.[1]

The name of Meghavarṇa, king of Ceylon, does not occur only in the Chinese text; it has been immortalised by the *Hitopadeśa.*[2] In the book III of that collection, after the seventh story, a guard announces "Meghavarṇa, king of the crows, who arrived from Ceylon, and now waits at the door with his followers". The story corresponding to *Pañcatantra*[3] (III, 1) also introduces Meghavarṇa, king of crows, but it assigns the residence of that person to the town of Mahilaropya in the Deccan. Besides, it gives him the role of a hero, whereas the *Hitopadeśa,* makes him a traitor. This double change does not appear to be due to a mere chance. The tradition gives to the king of crows a name quite appropriate of Meghavarṇa i.e. 'cloud-coloured'. But that name seems to have been one of the titles, preferred by the kings of Ceylon; Abhaya[4] bears it (254-

---

1 *J. R. A. S.*, 1890, p. 662.

2 *Hita upadeśa*--Instruction given through the medium of well-known fables. Name of a popular collection of fables intermixed with didactic sentences and moral precepts. This work is supposed to have been told by Viṣṇuśarman—B. C. Law.

3 Written by Viṣṇuśarman, containing didactic tales—B. C L..

4 Abhaya (Meghavaṇṇābhaya) same as Goṭhābhaya (302—15 A.D.)—*Mahāvaṃsa*, xv, 170; xxii, 11; xxiii. 10, 56; xxxvi, 58 etc.—B. C. L.

267), so also Kirtti-śri[1] (304-332), Amba Sāmaṇera Śilākāla[2] (526-539), Kirtti-śrī (560), Asiggāhaka[3] (614-623), Aggabodhi VI[4] (741-780) and Mahinda II[5] (787-807), Mahinda III[6] (812-816) and Sena I[7] (846-866). The Brahmin author of *Hitopadeśa* knew this well, and made an ingenious use of it; it tasted the favour of the Devil, to abuse the Buddhists of Ceylon, by reference to it. The crow is really the rebuke of the winged world, and its name implies metaphorically a shameless person. The episode appears to recall a mission sent to a king of India by one Meghavarṇa, probably the same mission was sent by Kīrtti-śrī Meghavarṇa to the Emperor Samudragupta, the king according to the mind of the Brahmins, who revived the old rite of *aśvamedha*. In any case, this explanation cannot be altogether rejected.

Ceylon and China

I give here the translation of the notes on Ceylon, printed in *Pien-i-tien*, chap. LXVI. I have also put forward along with it the extracts from Fahien and Hiouen-Tsang classified in the Chinese compilation under the T'ang and Tsin dynasties respectively. The memoirs of the two travellers are quite familiar to all the Indologists. The account of the eunuch ambassador Tcheng Houo, which finds place at the end of the chapter, relates to a time so modern that it should not be examined with the others. I preferred to set it aside in the sequence, and discuss it in part.

The first ambassador of Ceylon in China came at the time of T'sin; his mission does not form the subject matter of any

1 *Cūḷavaṃsa* lix, 42, 44; lxxiii, 136, 142.
2 *Ibid.*, xxxix, 48 ff.
3 *Ibid.*, xxxix, 44, 55; xli, 10 ff.
4 *Ibid.*, xlviii, 32.
5 *Ibid.*, xlviii, 42, 76.
6 *Ibid.*, xlix. 84 ff.
7 *Ibid*,, L, 1 ff; 43 (831-51 A. D.).
References 1-7 are supplied by B. C. L.

special account; it is simply noted in the History of the Leang. *Kao-seng-tchoan* written in 519, confirms the information given in official records on that mission:

"In olden times the king of Ceylon was as learned as Hiao-ou-ti (373-396) of the dynasty of Tsin, and was well-versed in law. He sent *cha-men* (*Śramaṇa*) *Tan-mo-I-iuen*, ordering him to offer respectfully a statue of the Buddha. Cha-men remained on the way for more than ten years, and arrived during the period I-hi (405-418)". The details relating to that statue agreed exactly with the *History of the Leang.*

Relations of Ceylon with China

(Pien-i-tien, ch. 66).

1st Part—Ancient times

Dynasty of the Soung—During the reign of T'ai tsou, in the fifth year Iuen-kia (428) the kingdom of Ceylon despatched a respectful address, and paid tributes.

The history of the Soung dynasty makes no mention of that fact in the section of T'ai tsou. But one finds it in the monograph of Ceylon:

In the fifth year Iuen-kia (428) the king Ts'a-li Mo-ho-nan (Kṣatriya Mahānāman) despatched a memorandum, which says, "I inform the illustrious lord of the great Soungs respectfully that although the mountains and the seas separate us, yet the news reach us from time to time. Prostrated before the august Emperor I hear of his virtue and of his ways, which are sublime and profound; he covers all like the sky, he supports all like the earth; he shines like the sun and the moon. Beyond the four seas, there is not any place where one cannot bow (before him); the kings of the countries do not fail to send their messages and to submit their respectful presents for showing you their sincere wish to share your virtue. As it floats very nearly for three years on the seas or moves along for thousands of days over the firm land, they have the fear of your prestige and love for your virtue. There is not a place so remote, from where people do not come. Our ancient kings, until now, considered as their unique duty to practise the virtue ; without being strict, they knew how to govern ; they served and honoured the Three Delights ; they directed and helped the people, and if the people behaved well, they were happy. As for me, I desired respectfully, in agreement with the Son of the Heaven, to enlarge the Good Law to save (the creatures) from the misfortune of transmigrations. That is why I order four priests (*tao-jen*) to offer Your Majesty two white robes and a statue with an ivory padestal, as a mark of my pledge of fidelity. I wish that your Majesty sends me a letter with his instructions for me."

In the seventh year *Iuen-kia* (430), the kingdom of Ceylon sent an ambassador, offering certain objects of the country—'It has been mentioned in the *History of the Soung*, in the section of Tai tsou. In the twelfth year *Iuen-kia* (435), the kingdom of Ceylon sent an ambassador, offering some presents from the country. Mention of this has been made in the *History of the Soung*, in the section of *T'ai tsou.*

Dynasty of Leang—In the third month of year *Ta-t'oung* (527) in the reign of Ou-ti, the kingdom of Ceylon sent an ambassador, offering presents from the country. It is in the section of Ou-ti in the *History of Leang*, the above account has been included.

The account of Ceylon says "The kingdom of Ceylon lies in the neighbourhood of India (*T'ien-tchou*). The country is agreeably equable without much difference in temperature between summer and winter. The five cereals are harvested there as they are sown, without waiting for a definite season. In the beginning, the country was not inhabited by men, but by demons and dragons. The merchants of the neighbouring countries, who went there for commerce could not see them ; they spread out precious articles and toys for sale on the ground indicating their prices ; the merchants bought the articles after the payment of prices, as indicated. The people of the neighbouring countries on learning about the wealth of the land hurriedly went there ; then went those, who settled there and founded later a great kingdom.

In the beginning of the period *I-hi* (405-418) of T'sin, were sent for the first time, as homage, a statue of jade and ten loads of written works (king=sutras ?). Now, as to the statue, it was four tch'eu (foot) and two ts'uenn (inch) high ; the form and the cut were absolutely extraordinary. Probably it was not the work of a human artist. During the entire periods of the reign of the T'sins and of the Soungs the statue was kept in the temple of Wa-koan; in the same temple there were five other statues of the Buddha, shaped by hand by Tcheng-cheu Tai Ngan-tao, and also the painting of Wei-wo (Vimalakīrti) by Kou Tch'ang K'ang. People used to call them the 'Three Wonders'. During the period of Ts'i, Toung-hoen (499-501) broke the jade statue; at first the shoulders were cut, then the body was taken for a woman of the second rank, who was his favourite, P'an; he made for her a pin for head-dress and a bracelet. In the Soung dynasty in the sixth year and in the twelfth of the Iuen-kia period the king Ts'a-li Mo-ho sent an ambassador to bring the tribute.

In the first year Ta-t'oung (527) a king of his lineage, Kia-che Kia-lo-ha-li-ya (Kāśyapa Kālahāryā ?) sent a letter respectfully.

The text of the letter is almost identical to the letter of Mahānāman, translated above, except the proper names.

T'ang Dynasty—In the third year Tsoung-tchang (670) during the reign of Kao-tsoung, the kingdom of Ceylon brought the tribe.

In the *History of the T'ang* there is no mention of that in the section of Kao-tsoung. But one reads as follows in the section of the 'Western Countries':

"Ceylon is situated in the middle of the south-western seas. Its length from north to south exceeds two thousands li. It is there that one comes across the mountain *Leng-kia* (Laṅkā). It abounds in rare wealth. Those treasures are spread out on the ground by the people of that country; the merchants, coming by boat, pay directly the equivalent sum and take them away. Next, the people of the neighbouring countries reached there by degrees, to settle, and they knew how to tame the lions; that gives the name of the country (Siṃha—'lion'; Siṃhala—'Ceylon'). In the third year T'soung-tchan they sent an ambassador to the court."

T'oung-tien of Tou (=ieou) says, under the authority of T'ou-hoan, that the kingdom of Ceylon is also named *Sin-tan*, and also *Po-lo-men*. It formed part of South India. In the north of the kingdom the inhabitants have the appearance of the Hous (barbarians of Central Asia); the autumn and the summer are hot and dry. In the south of the kingdom the inhabitants resemble the Leao (Laos). All the four seasons are rainy. Consequently they began to live in the temples of the Buddhist religion. The people have drooping ears, and they wrap cloth round their waists.

During the reign of Joui-tsoung in the second month of the second year King-iun (711) the kingdom of Ceylon sent goods from the country as presents.

The *History of the T'angs* does not mention it, nor the biographies, nor the monographs. It is from *Tch'e-fou-iuen-koe* that we come to know about it.

During the reign of Hiouen-tsoung, in the first year T'ien-pao (742) the kingdom of Ceylon sent an ambassador with certain articles of the country.

There is no mention of it in the section of Hiouen-tsoung in the *History of the T'ang*. The section on the Western countries says :

"In the beginning of the period 'T'ien-pao, the king *Chi-lo-mi-kia* (Śilamegha) sent on two occasions, an ambassador making an offer of presents of pearls, gold in filigree, stone collar, ivory, woollen cloth of fine texture and white colour (*pe-tie*)."

In the fifth year T'ien-pao (746) the kingdom of Ceylon sent men carrying their homage and presents to the Court. There is no mention of it in the *History of T'angs*, neither in the biographies, nor in the monographs. *Tch'e-fou-iuen koei* says :

"In the first month of the fifth year T'ien-pao the king of Ceylon, *Chi-lo-mi-kia* (Śilamegha) sent a monk of the Brahmin caste, *A-mo-kia-po-tche-lo* (Amoghavajra), master of *Tripiṭaka*, dispenser of the holy anointing, to the Chinese court, along with his homages, gold filigrees, precious stone collars, and, in addition, a copy of *Ta Pan-jo-king* (*Mahā-prajñā-pāramitā-sūtra*) written in Indian scripts (fan) on palm leaves, and forty pieces of white woollen cloth of fine texture."

In the third month of the ninth year T'ien-pao (750) the kingdom of Ceylon offered some ivory and pearls.

There is no mention of this in the *History of the T'angs*, neither in the biographies, nor in the monographs. It is in *Tch'e-fou-iuen-koei* that we come to know about this.

During the reign of Sou tsoung on the sixth lunar month

of the year 1 of Pao-ing (762) the kingdom of Ceylon brought to the court her compliments and tributes. *The History of the T'angs* does not make any mention of it, nor the biographies, nor the monographs. It is from *Tch'e-fou-iuen koei* that we come to know about it.

Appendix to the First Part

Vajrabodhi in Ceylon

Outside the official history, the name of the king *Chi-lo-mi-kia* (Śilamegha) of Ceylon occurs again in the biography of Amoghavajra (Soung-Kao-Seng-tchoan, chap. 1, p. 71a, Col: 17). The story of Vajrabodhi, master of Amoghavajra, interests equally the Sinhalese chronology. *Soung-Kao-Seng-tchoan*, *Siu kou-kin-i-king t'ou-ki*, and *K'ai-iuen chi-kiao-lou* contain biographical accounts of this personage; but the most authentic and precise account is furnished by *Tcheng-iuen siug-ting-i-kia mou-lou* compiled by Iuen-tchao in the beginning of the ninth century, and preserved only in the Korean edition. (ed. Jap. XXVIII, 6, chap. 14, p. 77-78). In the collection, catalogued by Nanjio, this important book has not been mentioned. The text of *Iuen-tchao* is taken and commented in the History of the tantric sect: *Wen-tcha-lo-kia-fou-fa-tchoan*, which I have brought from Japan. Vajrabodhi is the first son of a kṣatriya king of Central India, *I che-na-kia-mo* (Īśāṇākarman, corr. varman ?). If the other biographies described him as a brahmin of Mo-lai-ye (Malaya), it was because he went in the court with an ambassador of the country. I do not know which of the kings was Īśāṇakarman or varman; it is difficult to identify him with the king of the same name, mentioned in the inscription of Aphsad (*Corpus III.* no. 42), as the contemporary and unfortunate rival of Kumāragupta of Magadha, Vajrabodhi having been born in 661; Vajrabodhi studied at Nālandā until he was twenty six years old. Then he went on pilgrimage as far as Kapilavastu in 689 and proceeded immediately towards South-India, centre of the Avalokiteśvara cult. The kingdom of *Kien-tchi* (Kāñcī) was suffering for three years from an acute distress; the king *Na-lo-seng-kia-pou-to kia-mo* (Narasiṃha Potakarman, corr. Varman) begged the religious persons for help.

By means of the *dhāraṇīs*, Vajrabodhi brought rains. A vision directed him to visit Ceylon, and to worship Mañjuśrī in the Middle Kingdom. He went by sea and was received officially in Ceylon, and, there he worshipped the sacred relics, and particularly the Tooth, deposited at Abhaya-rāja-vihāra, where he stayed for six months ; then he left towards south-west, to climb up the Laṅkā-parvata. He stopped on his way at the stūpa of the ear of the Buddha, and arrived then in the village of Seven-Delights, and entered the kingdom of *Lou-ho-na* (*Rohaṇa*). The king of the country was an adherent of *Hīnayāna* ; Vajrabodhi lived one month for explaining him the great Vehicle (*Mahāyāna*). He reached then at the foot of the mountain ; it was a wild area, inhabited by wild men and extra-ordinarily rich in precious stones. After waiting there for a long time, he reached at the summit and contemplated the foot-print of the Buddha. From the height he saw on the north-west the kingdom of Ceylon, and beyond that the ocean. At the foot of the mountain, an enclosure of verdure was shaped like the rampart of a town ; the local people told him that it was the town of Laṅkā. The savages of the area presented themselves to pay respect to the Master. He took then the route to South India, and got a reception with as much honour and grandeur as during his first visit. He expressed a desire to the king to make arrangements for his departure to China, with a view to worshipping Mañjuśrī there and propagating the doctrine. The king dissuaded him at first, telling him about the difficulties on the voyage ; then he yielded to his entreaties and decided that an ambassador, in conforming to precedence, should go, taking presents for the emperor. He instructed the chief general *Mi-tsoun-na* to offer, on his behalf, a copy of the Sanskrit edition of *Mahā-prajñā-pāramitā*,[1] certain objects of art and pieces of cloth and perfumes.

1. Chinese *Hannya-haramitsu-kio*. The *Prajñāpāramitā sūtras* were preached by the Tathāgata for 22 years. All the *sūtras* belong to the so-called partially developed Mahayanism. (Yamakami, *Systems of Buddhist thought*, pp. 271-72). Nāgārjuna, the famous commentator on this *sūtra* says that faith is the entrance to the ocean of the laws of the Buddha and knowledge is the ship on which one can sail in it (*Ibid.*, p. 301).

The departure was carried out with great pomp. Vajrabodhi invoked Mañjuśrī on the east and Avalokiteśvara, westward. The mission took to the sea, and at the time of departure received greetings from the king, the ministers and the people. They first called at a port in Ceylon and in twentyfour hours' time the mission reached the port of *Po-tchi-li.* Some thirtyfive Persian boats already were there ; they had come for exchanging precious stones. When the Persian merchants saw Vajrabodhi, they followed him unanimously. The king of Ceylon, *Chi-li chi lo* (Śrī-Śila) on learning about the return of the master, invited him to live in his palace. After a month of sojourn, Vajrabodhi took leave of the king and departed, followed still by the faithful Persian merchants. After a month of sailing they reached at *Fo-chi* (Bhoja). The king came before the mission and presented him with a gold parasol and a gold bed. The end of the voyage was disastrous. All the boats of the merchants got scattered by a violent storm ; only the small boat, which was carrying Vajrabodhi touched at a port, after a long journey. It landed at Canton and proceeded towards the eastern capital, where it arrived in 720.

The Mahāvamsa and the Chinese Texts

The first Singhalese king, named definitely in the Chinese Annals is *ts-a-li Mo-ho-nan,* who submitted to the 'Son of the Heaven', a memoir, and some presents sometime in the year 428 A.D. *Tsa-li* is the usual transcription of the word, 'Kṣatriya'. As to *Mo-ho-nan*, we have already come across the name in the preceding pages, written exactly with the same letters, in the extracts from Wang Hiuen-ts'e where it stood for the Sanskrit name *Mahānāman.*[1] According to the computation of the *Mahāvaṃsa*, a king of that name in fact reigned from 412 to 434. Mahānāman, who was the younger brother of his predecessor Upatissa II, assasinated him after a reign of forty-two years and seized the throne ; immediately after that, he tried to forget

1 He ruled for 22 years (409-31 A.D.)—Malalasekera, *Dictionary of Pali Proper Names*, II, p. 516.—B. C. L.

his crime by observance of religious rites. It was during his reign that Buddhaghosa went to Ceylon from Magadha, who completed his great work of translation and the commentaries.[1] Desirous of establishing diplomatic relations with China, Mahānāman probably endorsed the scheme of the Singalese Church, which wanted to extend its field of action and to compete with the propaganda of the Indian Church. The visit of the traveller Fa-hien, who came to the island in 412-413, undoubtedly intensified the apostolic movement which united China with North India for more than three centuries. The commerce between the large island and a number of Chinese ports was already established *via* the ports of the Indian archipelago, and was regular and frequent. Fa-hien met before the Jasper statue in Ceylon, "a merchant who presented a form of white Taffeta brought from the country of Tsin". Even an ambassador had preceded the ambassadors of Mahānāman; unfortunately the Chinese documents have kept us ignorant of the name of the king, whom he represented, and of the exact date of his arrival. We know, however, that it was sent, attracted by the reputation of the emperor *Hiao-ou-ti,* who reigned from 373 to 396. The ambassador spent ten years on the way and reached China in the beginning of the *I-hi* period, which lasted from 405 to 418. He, therefore, could not reach before 395. In 396 *Hiao-ou-ti* died. The news of his death did not reach Ceylon at the time of the departure of the mission. Leaving in 395 or 396, or even a little later *Samaṇa Tan-mo-I-uen* was the representative of Upatissa II[2], who occupied the throne, according to the *Mahāvamsa,* from 370 to 412 A.D.

After an interval of thirty years, the two kings established contact with two different dynasties, Upatissa II, with that of Tsin, and Mahānāmān[3] with that of Soung. China, in fact, passed through a long period of confusion and political disruption; it was the time of 'kingdom making'. In 420, the southern Soungs defeated the Tsins, and captured, in their turn, *kin-ling*

---

1. His task was finished in three months (Law, *Buddhaghosa,* 1946, p. 10; Cf. *Mahāvamsa* (Turnour), pp. 250-253; *Cūḷavaṃsa,* PTS. 37 chap. vs. 215-246.—B. C. L.
2 *Cūlavaṃsa,* 41 Ch. verse 6.—B. C. Law.
3 *Mo-ho-nan.*

(Nankin) for capital. However, indifferent to the changes in dynasties, the Singalese remained faithful to the same region, the southern China.

New ambassadors arrived again between 430 and 435. The reign of Mahānāman ended in 434, according to the Sinhalese chronology. But the death of the king probably occurred when the last mission was already on its way. On the whole, the figures agree well on both the sides.

The official relations were again interrupted for about a century. It was again in 527 that a new mission arrived in China. They presented themselves in the name of the king *Kia-che Kia-lo-ha-li-ya*. *Kia-che*, as mentioned in the text, is the regular transcription of Kāśyapa. But Kāśyapa I[1] of the *Mahāvaṃsa* ruled from 479 to 497, and it is difficult to admit an error of thirty years, especially when it happened not long after Mahānāman. Kāśyapa II[2] is outside the picture, because he ascended the throne in 652. In 527 the king who ruled in Ceylon is named according to the *Mahāvaṃsa*, Amba-sāmaṇera Sīlākāla in Pāli, Ambaherana Salamewan in Singalese. Sīlākāla was the son-in-law of Upatissa III, who ascended the throne in 525[3] and was overthrown after one and half year's reign. Upatissa III had a son, Kassapa (Kāśyapa),[4] nicknamed Giri-Kassapa, who did not have any royal dignity, but who defended courageously the throne of his father against the enterprise of an ambitious son-in-law. One finds in the pages of the account of the Sinhalese chronology the following component parts of the royal name, as given in the *Annals of Leang*: *Kia-che* corresponds to Kassapa, son of Upatissa III; *Kia-lo* to Kāla, the component part of the name forming Sīlākāla; *Ho-li-ya* has a vague connection with the Sinhalese term *herana*. Two explanations are possible: it may be that the Pali annals have divided the name of one person, who would become later either the son, or the stepson

1 Pāli Kassapa who slew his father and became king of Ceylon as Kassapa I (A.D. 478 to 496)—B. C. L.

2 A.D. 641-650. He defeated Dāṭhopatissa and became king in his place.—B. C. L.

3 524-537 A.D. He reigned for 13 years—B. C. Law.

4 Kassapa was ultimately defeated by Silākāla and he fled to Merukandara with his parents and followers (*Cūlavaṃsa*, xli, 8-25).—B. C. Law.

of Upatissa III; or it may be that the Chinese have mixed up the information given on the two rivals, fighting for power, Sīlākāla on one side, and Kassapa, on the other. It must be remembered that it was again with the court of Kinling (Nankin) that the Sinhalese established diplomatic relations. The Leangs were overthrown by the Soungs and their successors, the T'sis, since 502.

The Annals do not give the names of the kings, who sent the missions between 670 and 711. According to the chronology of the *Mahāvaṃsa,* the king of Ceylon in 670 A.D. was Hatthadāṭha, also named Dāṭhopatissa II (664-673).[1] In 711 it was Māṇavamma[2], whose long reign extended from 691 to 726. The voyage of Vajrabodhi took place during his time; his two visits to Ceylon occurred between 705 and 715. But the king of South India, who gave reception in the first instance, also was taken notice of in the Sinhalese chronology. The *Mahāvaṃsa* tells us that the prince Māṇavamma, son of Kassapa II, and son-in-law of the king Malaya, pursued by his enemies, took service in the court of a king of India, Narasiṃha, who bestowed on his brotherly affection. The two princes are noted for their generosity and refinement. Another king of India, named Vallabha, attacked Narasiṃha in the meanwhile; Māṇavamma, who took part in the combat, caused Narasiṃha to win, and Narasiṃha, in recognition of that, entrusted an army to the prince of Ceylon to enable him to recover his throne. The first expedition failed; the second succeeded. Māṇavamma ascended his paternal throne and reigned for thirty-five years. An inscription of Vikramāditya Cālukya, great grandson of Pulakeśi, who vanquished Harṣavardhana, notes also the battle that raged between Vallabha and Narasīṃha: "Vanquished by the might of Śrī-Vallabha, who had squashed the glory of Narasīha...(Vikramāditya) vanquished on his return the Pallava (of Kāñcī[3]). The same Vallabha was a king, Gaṅga of Kaliṅga, according to another

1 650-658 A.D. (*Cūlavaṃsa,* xliv, 154). He was defeated by Māṇavamma and was killed. (Malalasekera, *Dictionary of Pali Proper Names,* Vol. II, p. 605).—B. C. L.

2 He reigned circa 676-711 A.D.—B. C. L.

3 *Indian Antiquary,* VI, 77.

inscription[1]; he won a victory over the Pallavas, which cost the life of the vanquished king. Lewin Rice has already attempted to identify that Narasiṃha with a king Narasiṃha Potavarman, who has been mentioned in an inscription of Kīrtivarman II, the Cālukya".[2] "He (Kīrtivarman) entered Kāñcī, without causing destruction......and offered a lump of gold to the temples of Rājasiṃheśvara etc. which Narasiṃha Potavarman had constructed in stone." The identity of the two persons becomes now evident; the accounts of the time, of the places, of the persons mentioned in the *Mahāvaṃsa*, the inscriptions and the biography of Vajrabodhi, all point to the same conclusion. Pallava Narasiṃha-Potavarman[3] of Kāñcī, therefore, reigned towards the end of the year 700.[4]

The king of Ceylon, who gave a reception to Vajrabodhi in his first travel, has nowhere been mentioned. But the mention of the kingdom of Rohaṇa as an independent State agrees well with the date given in the *Mahāvaṃsa.* The island, during that period, was a vast battle-field, where constantly clashed the rivals who disputed for power with furious obstinacy. The mountainous country of Rohaṇa, in the south, served as a place of refuge for the vanquished. The kings of Anurādhapura did not succeed to establish their authority there. During the reign of Dāṭhopatissa II (664-673) a certain Aggabodhi 'whose sister married the king of Rohaṇa'[5] made himself master of the whole of the country. His brother Sāmi Dappula, inherited the sovereignty and 'he became the chief of Rohaṇa'.[6] He married the daughter of the king Śilādāṭha[7] and had sons, Māṇavamma, etc. The same Māṇa (vamma) was defeated and killed by the

1 *Ibid.*, X, 37 No. 7.

2 *Ibib.*, VIII, 26.

3 The powerful Pallava king of Kāñcī who destroyed the Cālukya power. He was the most considerate potentate of the south. Narasimhavarman's capital was visited by Hiuen Tsang in 640 A.D. (V. A. Smith, *Early History of India*, pp. 472, 483).—B. C. L.

4 A.D. 625-45 according to V. A. Smith (*Early History*, 4th Ed., p. 495.)—B. C. L.

5 A province of Ceylon (*Mahāvaṃsa*, 22. vs. 6 and 8)—Law

6 For three years (650-53 A.D)—Law

7 *Cūlavaṃsa*, xlv. 16-22; 36 ff.; 51 ff. Dappula died being greatly sorrowful at the death of his son Māṇavamma who was killed by Hatthadāṭha—B. C. Law

men of Dāṭhopatissa ; his father then followed him in grave : "He reigned for seven days at Anurādhapura and three years at Rohaṇa."

Then, in his second voyage, Vajrabodhi was received by the king Śrī Śila (Siri-Sīla). The lists in the *Mahāvaṃsa* do not mention this name. It is impossible that Sīlamegha, who according to the *Mahāvaṃsa*, ruled in 741, could be the same person. It is likely that he was one of the short-lived kings who gained power, in turn, sometime in the year 700. The account in the *Mahāvaṃsa* confused the issue and lost the name ; it is, therefore, we turn to the history of Sāmi Dappula of Rohaṇa and find that the name of certain king Sīlā-dāṭha appears there, who is unknown otherwise. It is probable, and the hypothesis seems to be very plausible that Śrī Śila is a royal title (*biruda*) of the king Māṇavamma, the name invariably given to all the kings of Ceylon in that period. The prince Māṇavamma, ascending on the throne, took the title of Śrī Śila.

The two ambassadors of Sīlamegha do not cause any difficulty. One was dated 742, and the other, 746. They fall in the period assigned by the *Mahāvaṃsa* to Aggabodhi VI Sīlamegha, 741-78.[1] The ambassador of 750 and that of 762 were sent by the same king. With him ceased the official relations between Ceylon and China ; on the nature of this type of relation, however, there should be no illusion. These relations were not established due to some political considerations. They could hardly be taken to mean a perfect understanding between the two states. To pretend that the missions have always been authentic (and the Chinese emperors let themselves be deceived more than once by the impostors) does not have any other reason but vanity on the part of a king, keen to have his name known far away, or again the religious zeal cleverly exploited by the commercial interests. The story of the Persian merchants stubbornly following Vajrabodhi is well expressive. It is up to an author of edifying biographies to recognise in this move the prestige of a holy monk. The Persian merchants knew well that

1 He became king under the name of Silamegha (727-766 A.D.)—*Cūḷavaṃsa*, vs. 42, 60, 61, 76, 90.—B. C. Law

by following Vajrabodhi they got the protection of the mission and that they would be received well in the Buddhist countries. The international commerce soon made the best use of the politics of the missionaries.

To sum up, the Chinese texts enable us to check the chronology as given in the *Mahāvaṃsa* over a period of four and a half centuries, between the reign of Śrī Meghavaṇṇa and that of Aggabodhi VI Sīlamegha. Out of the six names of the kings clearly indicated, three names have been agreed upon by both the texts: the dates assigned by both the texts to Mahānāmam (fifth century), to Narasimha Potavarman (seventh to eighth century), to Aggabodhi Sīlāmegha (eighth century) coincide. In the other cases, there is some slight discrepancy. Śrī Meghavarṇa appears to have ascended the throne a few years later than the date indicated by the *Mahāvaṃsa*, the names of Kāśyapa Kalaharya VIth and of Śrī Śila (8th century) do not appear in the Pali Annals. But if we analyse the first of the two names, we shall come across the component parts in the corresponding period in the *Mahāvaṁsa*, and the second name is probably one of the royal titles taken, according to the usage, by a king, whose name only, without the title, has been retained by tradition. The apparent disagreement rather points out to perfect agreement in both the texts. One may very well conclude after this study that the chronology of the *Mahāvaṃsa* should be taken as an authority, if not unimpeachable at least from the fourth century.

Second Part—Modern Times.

Tcheng Houo and Ma Hoan. There are two accounts, which refer to the voyages of Tcheng Houo in the first half of the fifteenth century. While the Portugese sailors, under the patronage of Henry, the Navigator, rushed for the conquest of far off seas and unknown lands, a similar movement was happening in the other end of the world. The emperor Ioung-lo sent in 1403 his eunuchs to Tibet, Java, Siam and Bengal. In 1405 he entrusted the eunuch Tcheng Houo with the exploration of the Southern Seas; he gave him a fleet of 62 ships. Tcheng Houo made successfully seven expeditions in the course of thirty years. He pushed his adventurous course as far as the coast of Arabia. "He made captive, in turns, in his first expedition, the chief of Kiu-kiang, the ancient country of San-fo-tsi, in Sumatra; in a later expedition, the king *A-lie-kou-nai-eul* of Ceylon with his wives and children; finally in the last expedition, Su-kan-li, son of the king of Sumatra." The text which we have translated from *Pien-i-tien* does not give the precise dates of the voyages of Tcheng Houo to Ceylon, and his victory over the Sinhalese. But one can determine the date approximately. We know that this incident took place later than the first mission, which left China in 1405; and, on the other hand, that Tcheng Houo, conqueror of *A-lie-kou-nai-eul* returned in China in 1411. It appears from the account that nothing untowards happened on the way. It is, therefore probable that the episode occurred in 1410.

I add to the extract from *Pien-i-tien* a note borrowed from *Ing-iai-cheng-lan* of Ma Hoan. Ma Hoan was a Chinese muslim. He was attached as a interpreter to the mission of Tcheng Houo from the year 1413, because of his knowledge of the Arabic language. I could not get hold of original text of the account of Ma Hoan. I have been obliged to translate in French the English version given by Philips.[1] A document discovered by Mayers, which was not taken notice of by Philips, gives the date of the passage of Ma Hoan to Ceylon.[2] The vessels of Tcheng Houo touched at *Pie-lo-li*, the port of Ceylon, on the sixth day of the eleventh month of the seventh year of Siuen-si (at the end of 1432); they weighed anchor on the tenth day.

I

Pien-i-tien Chap. 66—*Sie-lan-chan* (island of Sie-lan) is the ancient kingdom of *Seng-kia-lo*. Near the palace of the king is to be found the tooth of the Buddha. It lies within a magnificent building, the stones of which shine like fire. For several generations it was worshipped continuously, and the ceremonies

1 G. Philips, *The seaports of India and Ceylon by Chinese voyagers of the fifteenth century*, *China Branch R.A.S.*, XX, 209-226; XXI, 30-42.

2 Mayers, *China Review*, III, 329.

did not fall in disrepute. At present the king is *A-lie-kou-nai-eul*. He is a *Souo li*. He observes the practices of the heresy, and does not respect the law of the Buddha. He is a tyrant, cruel and impetuous, who does not have pity upon the people of the kingdom, and who treats the tooth of the Buddha insolently. In the third year of Ioung-lo (1405) the emperor sent the eunuch, Tcheng Houo with flowers and perfumes to make devout offerings in foreign countries. Tcheng Houo invited the king *A-lie-kou-nai-eul* to worship the emblem of the Buddha, and to reject the heresies. The king was annoyed and wanted to punish him severely. Tcheng Houo came to know about that and left the place. Then, he intended to go to some other foreign country to offer presents and took some gifts for the king of the island of Sie-lan. The king, most arrogant, did not receive him well and even went as far as to mistreat him. Under his orders, 50,000 armed men felled trees to block the road; another army was sent to destroy the fleet. But it so happened that the subordinates of the king disclosed the plot. Tcheng Houo and his men hastened to reach their boats. The road was already cut. Tcheng Houo sent secretly messengers with the order to soldiers to disembark and not to give in to the enemies. With 3,000 men Tcheng Houo went at night by some unfrequented ways, and attacked the capital, and seized it. Then the barbarian soldiers who had gone to destroy the fieet and also the barbarian soldiers coming from the interior of the kingdom arrived on all sides, mustered, and surrounded the town and gave battle for six days. Tcheng Houo and his men, keeping the king as prisoner left at daybreak, clearing the trees which were cut to get to the road. They went for a distance of 20 li, sometimes fighting, sometimes marching. At night they arrived near the boats. Before embarking, they worshipped, following the rites, the tooth of the Buddha; and then they alone embarked. And then some supernatural wonder happened: people saw some light glowing, wherefrom a voice spoke (on the temple); the thunder-bolt roaring and lighting far away. They escaped unnoticed, surmounted all the obstacles and pushed onward over the sea for more than 10,000 li without being troubled either by the winds or by the waves, everything being smooth and quiet. The savage dragons and the wicked fishes appeared in front, pell-mell, but peaceful and without wishing any harm; and in the boats the men feeling security were happy. On the ninth day of the seventh month in the ninth year of Ioung-lo (1411) they reached the capital.

II

Ing-iai-cheng-lan, of Ma Hoan—(Leaving the Nicobar islands on the west), one sees the hill of Beak of Hawk at the end of seven days, and two or three days later one reaches the hill of the Buddhist temple; the anchoring of the port of Ceylon, called *Pie-lo-li* is quite close to it.

On landing, one can see on the bright rock, at the foot of the cliff, the impression of a foot which is two feet or more long. That print, according to legend, is that of the foot of Śākyamuni, when he had landed on that spot coming from the islands of T'sui-lan (Nicobar). In the hollow of the foot-print, there is some water, which never gets evaporated. The visitors dip their hands in the water, sprinkle the water on their faces and eyes saying "It is the water of the Buddha; it will make us pure and fit."

The Buddhist temples abound in that area. In one of the temples one can see a statue of Śākyamuni lying flat on the whole of its length, and which is still in a good condition.

The pedestal on which rests the statue, is inlaid by all sorts of precious stones. It is made up of sandalwood, and is very elegant. The temple contains a tooth of the Buddha[1] and other relics. It must be the place where Śākyamuni obtained *Nirvāṇa*.[2] At a distance of 4 or 5 li from that place northward, is situated the capital of the kingdom. The king belongs to the race of *So-li*, he believes with favour in the law of the Buddha; he treats the elephants and cows with respect. The men of the country are in the habit of taking cowdung, burning it, and when it is reduced to ashes they rub it on their body. They

1 Cf. *Dāṭhāvaṃsa*, which gives an account of the tooth-relic of the Buddha, written during the reign of king Kittisirimeghavaṇṇa (vide B. C. Law, Ed. 1925).—B. C. L.

2 Perfect beatitude. (Law, *Concepts of Buddhism*, 2nd Ed. Chap. XIII)—B. C. L.

do not eat beef; they drink simply water. When a cow dies, it is buried. It is a capital crime to kill a cow secretly. One can, however, escape punishment, if he pays as ransom a head of the cow in solid gold. Every morning the men of the royal house, whatever be their rank, take cow-dung, mix it with water, spread it on the ground at their residence; then they bow down and accomplish their religious rites. Near the residence of the king there is a mountain which rises to the sky. On the summit of this mountain lies a foot-print of a man, sunk in rock to a depth of 2 feet, and 8 feet or more long. It is said that it was the foot-print of the ancestor of mankind, a holy man, called *A-tan*, also known as *P'an kou.* The mountain abounds in rubies of all qualities, and in other precious stones. Those gems are continually separated from the soil by heavy showers of rain. People look for them and find them in sand heaps, transported lower down by the torrents. There is a saying among the people that the precious stones are the tears of the Buddha, now frozen.

There is in the sea, away from the coast ot the island, a sand-bank, which looks like snow. When the sun or the moon shines, it glitters brilliantly. The pearl-oysters accumulate continually on the bank.

The king had the ground dug to prepare an oyster-bed; every second or third year he puts fresh pearl-oysters and has it protected by special guards. Those who fish the oysters and bring them to the authorities for the use of the king, sometimes steal them and sell them as contrabands.

The kingdom of Ceylon[1] is big, densely populated, and resembles Java in certain respects. The people find there in abundance everything that one wants to have. They go naked except putting round their loins a piece of green cloth, fastened with a belt. They kept their bodies well shaved; they take care only of the hair of the head. They roll a piece of white cloth round their heads. If they lose their mother or father,

---

1 Vide Geiger's article, entitled *A Short History of Ceylou* (From the 5th century B.C. to the 4th century A.D.) published in B. C. Law, *Buddhistic Studies*, Chap. XXX, pp. 711-727—B. C. L.

they let their beards grow; it is, therefore, the sign of filial devotion. The women twist their hair and make a knot behind the head, they wear a white cloth round the waist. The head of the newly born male child is shaved; but nothing of that sort is done in a female child. They keep tuft of hairs till their adolescence. They must have with their meals plenty of butter and milk. They always chew betelnuts. They do not have wheat, but they have rice, sesame and peas. The cocoanuts which they raise in abundance, furnish them with oil, wine, sugar and nourishment. They cremate their dead persons, and bury the ashes. When there is a death in the family, it is the custom that the women of the parents and of other neighbours will meet and will beat their breasts by hand and at the same time will groan and lament loudly.

They reckon amongst their fruits, the banana and the bread fruit; they also have sugarcane, melons and garden crops and plants. The cows, sheep, fowls and ducks are also found in great numbers. The king has in circulation a gold coin, weighing 1.6 *candarin.* They like very much the Chinese musk, coloured taffetas and basins and cups made of blue porcelain, copper coins and camphor. They barter these against pearls and precious stones. The Chinese vessels, which return to China, always bring back the envoys of their king, carriers of precious stones as presents, offered as tributes to the imperial court.

The king, visited by Tcheng Houo at the time of his first visit to China, and who gave such a bad reception to the Chinese envoy, bears a name, which is easily recognisable under the Chinese transcription. *A lie kou nai eul* (A-le-ko-na-r) is the king who figures in the royal lists under the title of Bhuvaneka-bāhu V; before his accession to the throne, he was known under the name of Alagakkonāra.[1] He is a *Souo-li.* Ma Hoan describes also the king who reigned a little later in Ceylon; *Souo-li jenn tcheu*, 'Soli vir stippe'. Philips is of opinion that *Souo-li* comes from the Sanskrit transcription 'Sūrya', and proposes to explain this: The king is of Sūryavaṃśa. In fact the king contemporary to Ma Hoan is, according to *Mahāvaṃsa*, of the race of the Sun

1 *Mahāvaṃsa,* Chap. XCI, 2-13.—There is no such chapter in Geiger's *Mahāvaṃsa,* 1908—B. C. L.

(Chap. XCI, v. 16), but it is not so in the case of his predecessor Alagakkonāra. Besides, the name of *Souo-li*, written with the same letters, reappears in another passage in the book of Ma Hoan, which cannot have the same interpretation as that proposed by Philips. "The hand writing used in Java resembles that of *Souo-li*".[1] Mayers has interpreted it correctly "by the name of *Souo-li*"; says he, "that the inhabitants of the Malaya archipelago, mean the southern part of the Indian Peninsula to which the same name is given by Marco Polo. And it gives the same form to the Sanskrit word *Coḍa*. 'Soli' is, in fact, the term used in Sinhalese language, equivalent to the Sanskrit word, *Coḍa*. It is hardly necessary to refer to the constant connection between Ceylon and the Coḍas; it will not be surprising if the kings of Ceylon have come from Coḍa.

The king Alagakkonāra was at first prince of Perādoṇi, the modern Peradeniya is in the immediate vicinity of Kandy; but as he aspired to have the glory of founding a new capital, he chose a site to the south of Kelani, quite close to the sea, a little behind of Colombo, and there he built up the town of Jayavaddhanakoṭṭa, 'which was decorated with great ramparts, gates and turrets'.[2] One century later the Portuguese found the new capital in a prosperous condition. The accounts of the sixteenth and of the seventeenth centuries frequently mention it under the name of *Cotta*; the State, of which it was the capital, was known as the kingdom of *Cotta* and the king received the title of the 'emperor of Coṭta'. The colossal statue of the Buddha is still visible, as in the times of Ma Hoan, in the temple of Kelani, and the tourists, who make a short visit to Colombo, do not fail to go there to see it. I have not seen any foot-print, which was shown to Ma Hoan on the rock at the foot of a cliff; but this fact is in accord with the tradition of the *Mahāvaṃsa*, which relates in the first çhapter, the visit of the Buddha at Kalyāṇi (Kelani). Philips was not well versed in the history of Ceylon and therefore, interpreted wrongly, and even tried to correct the statements of Ma Hoan. In this opinion, the hill of

1 *China Review*, IV, p 179.

2 It became the capital of Ceylon (*Cūḷavaṃsa*, xci, 3-9)—B. C L.

Beak-of-Hawk stands on the coast of Batticalva, and the hill of the Buddhist temple in the promontory of Dondera in the extreme south of the island. Hence, he looked for the capital in the same region, behind *Belligamme,* where he expected to find the port of *Pie-lo-li.* I do not know which name corresponds to *Pie-lo-li* ; but it cannot be *Belligamme* (*Weligama*). The site is to be searched at Colombo or to its immediate environs. It is certainly the promontory of Dondera (*Devanagara*), which is the hill of Beak-of-Hawk of the Chinese navigators, and the hill of the Buddhist temples is the Lavinia hill. As to the second king, visited by Ma Hoan, it is certain that he was Parakkamabāhu VI[1], who ascended the throne at Jayavaddhanakoṭṭa in 1410 or 1415 and was the second successor of Bhuvanekabāhu V Alagakkonāra. Ma Hoan bears witness to his ardour of the Buddhist faith, which concurs with the account given in the *Mahāvaṃsa* ; but it is otherwise with his predecessor. Alagakkonāra, whom Tchen Houo represented as an arrant heretic, is exalted in the Sinhalese chronicle as a model of godliness. The king, whom the Chinese accused of treating with disrespect the tooth of the Buddha is according to the other text responsible for a casket to be made at a cost of 7,000 silver pieces for keeping certain precious relics. Has Tchen Houo slandered a dishonest host ? Or has the *Mahāvaṃsa* lied piously ? In any case the *Mahāvaṃsa* does not utter a word on the curious event, in which a Chinese eunuch appears as a forerunner of Vasco de Gama and of Almeyda.

Note on the fragments III & IV

The Hot Spring of Nepal

The hot spring of Nepal appeared to the Chinese as a striking feature. The *History of the T'angs* inserted in the Account of Nepal a fairly long description of this natural

---

1 He was the ruler of Jayavaddhanapura (*Cūḷavaṃsa*, xci, 16 ff.). As regards the date some place it at 1412 A.D. He restored the monasteries at Gaṇḍāladoni. He abdicated in favour of his sister's son Viraparakkamabāhu and died after a reign of 55 years. The Sinhalese poetry was very much encouraged in his reign. —B. C. L.

curiosity. Hiouen-Tsang also did not fail to add a note on this in his brief account of the same kingdom. *Fa-iouen-tchou-lin* again refers to it in another section, where he gives an abridged itinerary of India, based on Hiouen-Tsang and Wang Hiuen-ts'e and *Si-iu-tchi.* The latter description, without any change whatsoever, recurs again in *Chen-kia-fang-tchi* of Tao-siuen (compiled in 650). It is difficult to suppose a direct borrowing, because the itinerary of *Fa-iouen-tcheu lin* is, in all other matters, entirely independent of *Cheu-kia-fang-tchi.* Both the books might have drawn from the same common source, which must be the account of Wang Hiuen-ts'e. The translation of that passage is given below :

Cheu-kia-fang-tchi, Chap. I. p. 97. col. 13—*Fa-ïouen-tchou-lin,* chap. 29, p. 96, col. 14)—"To the south-east of the capital, at a little distance, there is a lake full of water and of flame. Proceeding for a distance of one *li* eastward, one comes across the spring, *A-ki-po-li* (Fa-iouen says : *A-ki-po-mi* ; the same alternation as in the two editions of the *History of the T'angs.*

The circumference of that lake is 20 *pou* (40 paces). The water is deep both in the dry season and in the rainy season. The water does not flow, but it always boils. If one holds a lighted candle by hand, the whole of the lake is set on fire ; the fume and flame rise upward to several feet. If one sprinkles water on the fire, it becomes more intense. If one throws powdered earth in it, the flame disappears, and everything that one puts in a pot above the water with a view to cooking food, is cooked well. Formerly there was in that fountain a gold casket. A king ordered that it should be taken out. When an attempt was made to take it out of the mire, the men and the elephants failed to tow it. And at night a supernatural voice said : "Here lies the crown of Maitreya Buddha ; none can take it out, as the Nāga of Fire guards it."

To the south of the town, at a distance of more than 10 *li,* stands an isolated mountain, covered with dense vegetation. There are many temples of several storeys, which appear like a crown of the clouds, under the pine trees and bamboo groves, the fishes and the dragons follow men, tamed, and without any fear. They approach men and get from them food to eat. Whosoever strikes them causes his own ruin. Lately the orders of the Empire faded out of the kingdom, and spread elsewhere in distant lands. Now, it is dependent on *Tou-iouen-tchou-lin.* (*Fa-iouen-tchou-lin* substitutes the latter statement by "On the east, the kingdom of Women is adjacent to *Tou-fan*"). *Chen-kia-fang-tchi* gives a hint, immediately before the passage, common to both the texts, coming undoubtedly from the same source and being of sufficient interest :

"In the capital city (of Nepal) there is a storied building, which is more than 200 *tch'eu* (foot) high, and 80 *pou* (400 feet) in circumference. Ten thousand persons can live in that building. It is divided into three terraces, and each terrace is further sub-divided into seven storeys. In the four pavilions, there are many wonderful sculptures, inlaid by pearls and precious stones."

I have travelled widely in the valley of Nepal for two months without coming across a spring of that type ; everyone whom I questioned, denied its existence. An amazing phenomenon of that sort should not fail to attract superstitious respect from the inhabitants of the valley, be they Gurkhas or Nepalese. There is nothing, neither a temple nor a chapel which can refer to a similar wonder. If the information given by the Chinese be correct, and there is no reason to doubt its authenticity especially when Hiouen-tsang and Wang Hiuen-ts'e said the same thing, supported by Li-I-piao, we are forced to conclude that an earthquake, as it still recurs in the Himalayan region, caused inflammable fountain to disappear.

Moreover, if on this point the correctness of Wang Hiuen-ts'e be doubted, we may take some hint from a hot spring situated on the Tibetan borders. I have come to know from the father of Captain Bhairav Bahadur, orderly officer of the Maharaja, that the spring really exists near the Tibetan frontier, on the route to Lhasa from Khatmandu. My informer, who held the post of Nepalese Resident at Lhasa, has, like the Chinese envoy twelve centuries before him, cooked his rice, on the spring, on his way. Tibetan passers-by never fail to halt there to do the same thing. It appears that there exists near the spring a number of inscriptions in Chinese, Tibetan and Sanskrit. It will be long before an European will reach at that spot to restore them. They promised me to send soldiers to that place for taking impressions in accordance with my instructions, but inspite of the steadfast kindness of the Nepalese government, I have received nothing from that source. It appears that the place named *Pyang pheḍi* corroborates again the statement of Wang Hiuen-ts'e, because *pheḍi* means a 'depression' and the Chinese indicated clearly that it was in a depression that the spring was encountered.

The mountain, situated in the south of the capital, at a distance of 10 *li*, appears to me identical with the holy mountain of *Sambhunāth*, also called *Svayambhū*. From the foot of the *Sambhunāth* to the plateau which contains Hirigaon, and where stands the capital of the Thakuris, the distance is about 5 kilometres, equivalent to 10 *li* of our text. The hill, which contains the celebrated sanctuary appears to be completely isolated from a group of mountains which enclose the valley. It still retains the verdant aspect of the ancient times. The bushy vegetation covers its slopes, and conceals under its shade a large number of small chapels, mostly in ruins. The plateau contains an ancient *stūpa*, crowned by a golden spire, which dominates the foliage, and which can be seen from all the surrounding countries, with a town of temples and statues, where live many faithful Nepalese and Tibetans. No fish is found there; the only animals that live there are the monkeys. But without going far from the Sambhūnāth, we may see something in modern Nepal, which must have impressed the Chinese envoys. To take an example, at Choṭā Bālāji at the foot of the same mountain, there is a splendid reservoir filled with pure water, where live a large number of fish getting their food from the faithful. In the hut near the entrance people sell a kind of dry herb, which is liked very much by the fish as a dainty food; if one throws a handful of that into water, the fish appear in swarms, hasten towards the edges and often follow with a greedy and submissive look of the visitors who feed them. The unemployed Tibetans move about, with loud laugh, before the scene, which does not make them fatigued. S. Exe. Deb Shamsher, brother of the Maharaja, provided an opportunity for me to see such a scene in the lake of Rāṇī Pokhrī, close to Khāṭmaṇḍu.

As regards the building described by Wang Hiuen-ts'e I

should think that it was similar to that of *Khasa-caitya* at Budhnath. That temple is used today as a dwelling house for the Tibetans who come down to Nepal in winter, and which, rather dangerous to be examined minutely (I have had a bad experience), is formed mainly of three wide terraces, arranged in tiers, and which contains a vast hemisphere of plaster, crowning a pyramid and a turret; the total height is about 150 feet. A considerable number of faithfuls are spread on the galleries; a vivid and correct description of which given by Oldfield (*Sketches from Nepal*, II, 260), shows that they were arranged in groups on each floor.[1] According to a tradition the building of the *caitya* (shrine) was constructed by the king Māndeva, of whom we have several inscriptions and who reigned in the beginning of the sixth century. An inscription of Aṃśuvarman, which I found at Hirigaon, assigned the income of an estate for the maintenance of the *vihāra*[2] constructed by Māndeva. Another *vihāra* (monastery) attributed also to Māndeva, the Chakra-vihār, still exists at Patna. The *vihāra* of Budhnath must have been situated in the suburb of the capital, as it is not very far from Deo Patan, the site of a former capital. In any case, if it is not the same structure, the building described by *Cheu-kia-fang-tchi* was very likely of the same style.[3] I do not want to persist on the 'wonder' of the Chinese at the sight of the sculptures which decorate the pavilion; the history of the contemporary Nepal is to be studied very carefully so as to obtain fresh information on this point.

Note on the Fragments V and XI

The Monasteries of Kapiśa[4]

The Hanas and the Yue-tchis

I have already translated the relevant passage from *Si-iu-tchi* in the *Journal Asiatique* (1897, II, p. 529 and rest); but I think

---

1 See also the description, though not so correct, given by Wright in his *History of Nepal*, p. 100. I myself have taken a number of photographs at Budhnath.

2 Vide Law, *Geography of Early Buddhism*, Appendix, p. 74 ff.

3 The *Vaṃsāvali* mentions in the same period the construction of a palace of nine storeys by the king Śivadeva (Wright, p. 124).

4 Kapiśa is Chinese *Kia-pi-shi* which is the Capissa of Pliny and the Caphusa of Solinus. According to Ptolemy it was situated 155 miles north-east from

that it is necessary to take it up again here for discussing the details. The monastery of the ancient King, where Wang Hiuen-ts'e lived in 661 is mentioned by Hiouen-Tsang (Mem. I, 53). The other monasteries named in *Si-iu-tchi* have also been described by Hiouen-Tsang ; the traveller, *Ou K' ong*, who visited the same region between 760 and 744, a century after Wang Hiuen-ts'e, gives the names of several monasteries but those are not sanskrit names ; they are very likely Turkish names. The convent of ancient king is the monastery of the king *Yen-ti-li d'Ou-k' ong.*[1] The convent of the King, with its milk-tooth of the Buddha is described under the same name by Hiouen-Tsang (Memoir, I, 53). The convent of the wife of the king (Hiouen-Tsang *Ibid.*) is the convent Pin-tche d'ou-k'ong which recalls the title of Pin-tcheou, given to the queen of the kingdom of Women, Niu-Wang.[2]

The monastary of the Hans now remains to be mentioned. The relics which have been kept there, according to *Si-iu-tchi*, are exactly those which Hiouen-Tsang saw in the convent of the ancient king. But the origin, attributed to it, may be traced to a tradition, reported by Hiouen-Tsang, on the subject of a convent enigmatically mentioned in the *Memoirs* under the name of *Jin-Kia-lan* (I, 42) and of *Cha-lo-kia* in the Biography (I, 71 and 75). Both the names are equally irreducible from sanskrit origin. The sound *Jin* is represented by the ideogram of man ; hence Julian proposed to restore its original Sanskrit

---

Kabul. Julien supposes this place to have occupied the Panjshir and the Tagao valleys in the north border of Kohistan. According to Hiuen Tsang this country was 4000 li in circuit (Watters, *On Yuan Chwang*, I, p. 122). It produced various kinds of cereals and fruit trees. The inhabitants of the place were cruel and violent by nature. The language was rude. They used gold, silver and copper coins. The Kṣatriya king of the place loved his subjects. Every year he used to make a silver statue of the Buddha 18 ft. high and convoked the *mokṣamahāpariṣad*, an assembly where alms were given to the poor. There were convents, dagobas, monasteries and deva-temples. Vide Beal, *Buddhist Records of the Western World*, I, 54 ff.—B. C. Law.

1 *Journal Asiatique*, 1895, II, p. 357.

2 *History of the T'angs*, quoted by Bushell in his *Early History of Tibet in J.R.A.S.* n.s., XIV. 582.

as 'Nara-saṃghārāma'. But *Jin-kia-lan* and *Nara-saṃghārāma* appear to have the same meaning because of some graphical error. The Chinese and Japanese editions write: *ta-kia-lan* i.e., a 'grand monastery'. The character *ta* by a simple error became easily *Jin* in the manuscript of Julien. The characters *Cha-lo-kia* do not have at the same time their Chinese renderings; hence the interpretation becomes difficult. The two latter characters *lo-kia* are those that also occur in the name of the mountain *Tan-to-lo-kia*. We have said that it corresponded to *laka* in Sanskrit. Besides, that name of *Tan-to-lo-kia*, occurring in the same region as *Cho-lo-kia*, makes the matter more puzzling. The charecter *cha* represents, in the learned transcriptions, the sibilant cerebral ṣ; it does not serve any useful purpose except where some old tradition imposes it, as for example in *cha-men*, 'samaṇa' or rather, 'samaṇa' for 'śramaṇa'. But 'Ṣālaka' has nothing Sanskrit in it. We may think of śalākā, which means the tickets for the distribution of food among the monks of the same convent, similar to our 'bread coupons'. The room, where food is distributed, is known as 'śalākāsthāna'. We may refer in support of this interpretation, first to the confusion that invariably occurs between sibilant cerebral and the palatal (*Keṣa* or *Kośa*, *śaṇḍa* or *Ṣaṇḍa* etc.), and secondly to the fact that the Chinese king, founder of the monastery "left there already considerable wealth for the use of meritorious works" (Biogra—p. 73), and who loaded the monks with benefits (*Ibid.*, 72). It was a pious work in instituting similar distributions. But the hypothesis is still vague and nothing positive has yet been put forward. It is very probable that the name of the 'monastery of the Hans,' mentioned in *Si-iu-tchi* corresponds to *Tchen-tan-hou-li* of Ou-K'ong. 'Hou-li' appears to be the translation in Turkish of '*vihāra*'.[1] As regards the word Tchen-t'an, I have discussed its meaning in the Miscellaneous works of Harlez (p. 182 and sub), where I showed that it corresponded to *Cīna-sthāna* Cīn (a) tthān (a) or 'China' and furthermore to the title of *devapntra*, 'Son of God'. In fact, the Chinese origin of the monastery is doubtful, the disagreement between Hiouen-tsang

1 Cf. *J.A.*, 1895, II, p. 389.

and *Si-iu-tchi*, does not even imply two divergent traditions. The official compilers of *Si-iu-tchi* felt repugnance at the idea of reporting the history of the Chinese king kept as a hostage by the *Yue-tchis*, and hence represented the prisoner as an official envoy. It is also probable that they borrowed from Wang Hiuen-ts'e or from some other travellers the tradition that they adopted.

Founded for the *Yue-tchis* either by an hostage or by a Chinese envoy, the monastery of the Hans links up, in a vulgar memorial a Indo-scythian name with that of a Chinese. It recalls in our mind the voyage of the enigmatic king, who is considered as the first propagator of the Buddhist texts in China. I have discussed this tradition in the *Journal Asiatique* (1897, I, p. 14 and in subsequent pages). Specht has drawn the attention of the scholars to my article[1], and have put them on guard against my translation and interpretation. The new texts that I have collected and that I put forward here will enable impartial scholars either to accept my interpretation or that of my learned colleague.

The discussion till now rests essentially on a passage in *Wei-leao*, '*Abridged History of the Weis*', quoted in an annotation of *San-kouo-tchi*, and in other compilations. Unfortunately the text, as it presents itself, swarms with uncertainties and obscurites. The author, in reference to the introduction of Buddhism in China relates that a person of the name of *King* established contact with a king of the Yue-tchis of 2 B.C. But was the Chinese received by the Yue-tchis, or did he simply supply them with the Buddhist *sūtras* ? This question, appears at first sight as an idle talk : it has, however, a considerable importance. The conversion of the Yue-tchis is involved in the solution of the problem, and the conversion of the Yue-tchis dominates the history of Buddhism ; it marks a new phase.

To solve the difficulties about this important text, Specht takes the help of the three books, published subsequent to *San-kouo-tchi*, in the ninth, tenth and twelfth centuries respectively. I have come across four new quotations in the books, written in the seventh century. Their testimony is of considerable importance as they were written between 624 and 640. The above

1 *Journal Asiatique*, 1897, II, p. 166.

four references deviate considerably from all the texts reproduced in the notes on *San-kouo-tchi* ; they also differ appreciably from each other. Fa-lin the controversialist, gives in the same book at an interval of several pages two independent sections ; the one (P') is identical with that given by Tao-siuen (K) ; the other (P) is somewhat similar to that of Ien-tsoung (T). But if T is generally in verbal agreement with P, it deviates from the latter in the disposition of the parties who composed the account, and reproduced on the contrary the same sequence as 'P' and 'K'. It puts forward like them, the information about Cha-liu before writing anything about the Buddha. On the other hand, it is the only record that mentions the name of the period of the reign of Ngai-ti, when king established contact with the Yue-tchis. Three others (K.P.P') say more vaguely : "In time of Ngai-ti of the first Hai". On the other hand, it omits an important detail given only by P and ends like 'P' and 'K'. T, therefore, constitutes a sort of mixed collation of texts. On the whole, the first collation furnished by *Pien-tchen-loen* (P), appears to me to be in a position to guarantee authenticity ; it is that, which comes nearer to the text given in *San-kouo-tchi.* I have reproduced in italics all the words common to both the collations. In conclusion it may be said that it inserts in reference to Cha-liu such a historic indication, which has not been mentioned elsewhere, and which could not have any other origin but *Wei-leao* itself. In reference to that strange Cha-liu, which resembles Lao-tzeu, it adds.

"Not long while ago, the Bonnets—Jaunes, seeing that he had a head, completely white, gave to that Cha-liu the title of Lao-tan (Lao-tzeu) ; and they could defraud in safety and betrayed China."

The revolt of Bonnets—Jaunes broke out in 184 and continued during the troubled period, when ended miserably the Han dynasty. The Wei dynasty succeeded in certain parts of the territory, and also ended in its turn in 264. The author of *Weo-leao*, who, according to a recent finding of Hirth[1], wrote his treatise anytime between the two extreme dates 264 and 429,

---

1 *China and the Roman Orient*, p. 14.

must have been a contemporary of Wei, as he applied to an episode in the revolt of Bonnets-Jaunes, an expression *king cheu* i.e., "in the last generations", 'in that century'.[1]

A glance at the following table indicates clearly the relationship between the different collation of texts and their connection with the text given in *San-kouo-tchi.*

Insert p. 454 to Pien-tcheng-loen—chap. 5 (XXXVII, 8, 44 wei, Chinese "456 etc. etc. etc. etc.

"In the abridged edition of the *wei* we find in the chapter on the western countries: The king of *Lin-i* did not have a son. He, therefore, made offerings to the Buddha. His wife *Mo-ie* (Māyā) saw in the dream a white elephant[2] and she became pregnant. And a son was born to him.[3] On leaving the right womb, he came into the world spontaneously. His neck was upright; shaking the ground he marched seven paces.[4] As he had the appearance of a Buddha, and as he was born by the grace of the Buddha, he was given the name of Buddha. In the kingdom (of Lini T, P, K) there was a saintly person, named Cha-liu (what one tells about him, is to be found: P. K). Being very aged, he had white hair, and he resembled Lao-tzeu. He instructed the people constantly (the men T. P. K) on the subject of the Buddha, If any calamity befalls to men, i.e., as for example, if one does not have a son, he asks them to do penance and rituals to the Buddha; and to part with all they possessed to atone for their sins. Not long ago, the Bonnets-Jaunes on seeing that he was all white, gave to that Cha-liu, the title of *Lao-tan*; they could defraud in safety and betray China. In the time of Ngai-ti of the first Hans (in the period Iouen-cheou-T), Ts' in king went (was sent T. P. K) to the kingdom of the

1 Cf. I-tsing, *A Record etc.* trans. Takakusu, p. 184, in which are referred as *kin*, i.e., 'contemporary' relatively to 'ancient times' and to 'middle-ages', the persons that lived about a century back.

2 Six tusked white elephant.—B. C. L.

3 Cf. *Lalitavistara*, Ch. 3; *Mahāvastu*, Vol. II, p. 1; *Saundaranandakāvya*, II, 48 śloka—B. C. L.

4 Cf. *Lalitavistara*, Chap. 7, 86—He said, "I am born for the good of the world and for the spread of knowledge."—B. C. L.

Yue-tchis. Their king gave an order to his son, the heir-apparent, to communicate verbally the holy books of the Buddha (to king T. P. K). In returning to China what he said about the Buddha was in perfect agreement with the books of Tao (And it is how the doctrine of the books of the Buddha reached early to the first Hans, (T. P. K).

To fix up the text of this important passage it is necessary to take into account with regard to four of our quotations from the writing mentioned in *San-kouo-tchi*.
Insert Chinese here (p. 457).

"Kingdom of *Lin-eul.* The sacred literature of the Buddha says : The king of the kingdom begot the Buddha. The Buddha was heir-apparent. The name of his father was *Sie-t'eou* (Śuddhodana) his mother *Mo-ie* (Māyā). The Buddha had his body and dress of yellow colour. The back of his neck was blue like a piece of blue silk, his breasts, blue, and his hair copper-red. At first Māyā saw in a dream a white elephant, and she became pregnant. He came out of the right womb of his mother and, was thus, born ; he had then a knot. Shaking the ground he could march for seven paces.[1] That kingdom is situated in India, the capital is the centre of India.

Moreover, there was a holy person, named *Cha-liu.* In former times, in the first year of the *Iouen-cheou* period of Ngai-ti of Hans, king-lou, the chief scholar of the Imperial College, was sent to the Great Yue-tchis in a mission. He preserved, having received it orally, the sacred literature of the Buddha which said, "The second founder, it is that person". In the sacred books that he brought *lin pou se* (?) *sang men pe wenn chou wenn pe chou wenn pi-k'iu cheng men* are all the titles of disciples. The Buddhist books that he related, accorded completely with the Chinese books of *Lao-tzeu.*

When compared with others, the text given in *San-kouo-tchi* appears clearly as altered and mutilated, it contains some details, which do not occur elsewhere about the person of the Buddha, about the name of his adepts, about the precise year of the

1 This portion is a repetition—B. C.L.

voyage of *King-lou*,' about the supposed location of Kapilavastu[1] in the centre of India. But it omits the information, so singular and true on the whole, on the Buddhist cult before the Buddha Śākyamuni, on the sacrifice of propitiation offered by Śuddhodana, and on the origin of the name of Buddha ; it makes mention of *Cha-liu*, but it lets slip the curious episode which justifies the above name, and which attaches the memory of the holy person to the history of intense feuds in China during the 2nd century. The passage, which describes the relations of King (lou) with the *Yue-tchis*, is so hazy that it lends itself apparently to many contradictory interpretations. The disorder appeared to have increased gradually and towards the end it became as clear as moon. The words *feou-t'ou king chou ts'ai* hang in the air, to reappear at the beginning of the following phrase, where it arrays logically with the continuation.

The kingdom of *Lin-eul*, or by a slight modification of the second character *Lin-i* derives its name from the garden of *Lumbinī*, where was born the Buddha. In fact it is necessary to substitute for the modern reading *Lin-eul* the ancient pronunciation *Lin-ni* because the characters *lus*, really *eul* are capable of being represented by *ni-* in the transcriptions. The name of the famous garden has been represented well in the Chinese as *Loung-pi-ni*, *La-fa-ni*, *Lin-pi-ni*. One also comes across the abridged form *Lin-pi*. In the usual transcriptions of the word, representing the sound *Lin*, it is used with the character, which signifies "wood", "forest". The translators intended clearly by this contrivance

1 Chinese *Chia-Wei-lo-yueh*. It was the capital of the Śakyas among whom the Buddha was born. Kapilapura, Kapilāhvayapura were its different names (*Lalitavistara*, p. 243 ; p. 28). Kapilasyavastu is another name (*Buddhacarita*, I, v. 2). The famous Rummindei Pillar marks the site of ancient Lumbini garden the traditional scene of Śakyamuni's birth. V. A. Smith identifies it with Piprāwā in the north of the Basti district of the Nepal frontier. Rhys Davids takes Tilaura kot to be the old Kapilavastu. Some have identified it with Tilaura two miles north of Tauliva, the headquarters of the provincial government of Tarai and 3½ miles to the south-west of the Nepalese village of Nigliva, north of Gorakhpura situated in the Nepal Tarai. Rummindei is only 10 miles to the east of Kapilavastu and two miles north of Bhagavānpura. Cf. *Mahāvastu*, I, 348 ff. For details vide Law, *Historical Geography of Ancient India*, p. 90.—B. C. L.

to combine the idea and the sound in the transcription. The author of *Wei-leao* is hazy about this; without suspecting that *Lin-ni* represents a garden, he applied the name to the kingdom of Kapilavastu; he also betrays his superficial knowledge of Buddhism. He appears to have understood that other Buddhas had preceded Śākyamuni; he represents Śuddhodana as the admirer of the past Buddhas. As to *Cha-liu*, he appears to have known it, or at least to have recalled it in reference to an incident of the revolt of the Bonnets—Jaunes. The brief notice given in the chapter on the countries of the west gives rather a fuller account than what is given in *Wei-leao* in the section of 'political history'. In fact that revolt, about which we came to know from *San-kouo-tchi*, is entirely pervaded by magic. The chief of the mutineers, Tchang Kio, "made a particular study of the books of Hoang-ti, and of Lao-kiun (or Lao-tzeu) which deal with magic." He claimed to have received from a sage, who was looked upon as a man of wonderful powers, a book containing marvellous recipes.

The war started in 184; Tchang Kio obtained a number of garrisons with the help of magic papers and enchanted water; he even communicated his supernatural power to the messengers, who propagated his system and reputation. Later, the brother of Tchang Kio, besieged by the imperial troops, produced by a magical artifice a thunderstorm and caused a black cloud to descend from the sky, quite full of heroic warriors. Undoubtedly, Taoism and Buddhism contested for having the honour of providing for the chiefs of the rebellions their supernatural powers. The quarrel of competition between the two sects revived under each pretext. *Wei-leao*, in this case, decided in favour of Buddhism.

I attempted to show in a preceding memoir that *Cha-liu* was probably the common transcription of the name of Śāriputra (Prakrit *Sariyat*); I have given reasons which prompted me to put forward that interpretation. I would like to add that, according to Fa-hien, the Indian monks erected, whenever they settled, towers in honour of Śāriputra, Maudgalyāyana[1] and

---

1 At the time of the Buddha Gotama Sāriputta was known as Upatissa and Maudgalyāyana (Pali Moggallāna) as Kolita. They were born in a brahmin

Ānanda,[1] and in a parallel way in honour of *Abhidharma*, the *Vinaya* and the *Sūtra* : Śāriputra and *Abhidharma*, are classed in the first rank. On the use of the character *cha*, intended to represent a sibilant other than the cerebral, I can quote the name of the king *Bimbisāra*,[2] transcribed *p'ing-cha* (the same character as *Cha-liu*) in a translation made by Tchi exactly in time of the Weis (223-253). The traditional forms *cha-men, pi-cha-men* for the Sanskrit 'Śramaṇa', 'Vaiśravaṇa', show the same method, before the period of transcriptions by scholars of reproducing a non-cerebral sibilant. It so happens, in different examples, that *Cha* is used to represent : sibilant—*ar*, the 'r' being mobile in the middle of a syllable in Sanskrit. Why was Śāriputra represented in the character of an old person ? Probably to give him a venerable appearance. In a collection of Buddhist images that I have brought from Japan, and which, generally speaking, represented the ancient models, as preserved in the country of Nara, Śāriputra comes first of the series of six disciples, with the note : *tcheu-hoei ti i*, 'the foremost in wisdom (*prajñā*)'. The skull is raised very high, and is entirely bare, the eye-brows are thick ; the left hand is turned towards the shoulder, holding a stem with a leaf in its upper end, and which lies on the open right hand. The ears are very long, shorter, however, than those of *Tathāgatas*,[3] whose

---

family. Giving up household life they became the followers of the Wanderer Sañjaya. They left him and were instructed in Buddism They became *arahats* (saints). Among the disciples of the Buddha who acquired knowledge Sariputta stood pre-eminent and Moggallāna acquired supernatural knowledge. Among the debators Sariputta was eminent and could get the better in any argument (Rhys Davids, *Gotama the Man*, p. 109). Moggallāna was a very psychic man and valued much Āḷāra's methods (*Ibid.*, p. 110). Mrs. Rhys Davids further says that Moggallāna might have done much to give help to many with his great unusual gift of will-power (*Ibid.*, p. 158).—B. C. L.

1 Ānanda was born in the family of Amitodana. He was ordained in Buddhism by the Buddha. After Buddha's passing away he became an *arahat* (saint). B. C. L.

2 Bimbisāra was the king of Magadha. He met the Buddha. He was a staunch follower of the Buddha and became his disciple (*Vinaya-Mahāvagga*, I, 22). He gave many presents to the Buddha in the rest-house built by him (*Dhammapada-aṭṭhakathā*, Pt. III, p. 439).—B. C. L.

3 Meaning those who have trodden the right path. Vide Lord Chalmer's useful article entitled *Tathāgata* in *J.R.A.S.* 1898, 391 ff. See also Prof. Walleser's learned article on the origin of the Tathāgata in the journal, Taisho University, 1930.—B. C. L.

ears almost touch the shoulder. This characteristic feature, in any case, confuses it with *Lao-tzeu*, or rather *Lao-tan* as he was named in the passage "Lao with ears drooping."

The different appelations of the disciples of the Buddha, mentioned in the text, have been derived from Sanskrit words. *Pi-k'iu* is the common transcription of *bhikṣu*, as *cheng men* and *sang-men* are from *śramaṇa*. The expression in which occur the word *wenn* i.e., 'to-hear' (*pe-wenn, pe-chou-wenn*) are translations probably of 'Śrāvaka' (the listener) ; it is probably the same with *Choa-wenn*, where the letter *wenn* signifies 'to interrogate'. As to the syllables, *lin pou se* I do not find any explanation : I only observe that the publication of Shanghai, which I abridged, does not have the term *i-pou-se*, which Specht borrowed from the compiler of *T'oung-tien* and not from the original text of *San-kouo-tchi*, and based on this he argues that the letter 'i' stands for the Sanskrit '*u*'. I do not want to enter into a controversy on this point, but I must make it quite clear, so as to forewarn the reader against a clear error, that the letter to which Specht has given here the meaning *pa*, only figures in transcriptions as the labial mute letters along with *u* or better still o[1], and never represented by *pa*, short or long in Sanskrit.

I would like to add a few more new details which I have already collected, on the *Yue-tchis*. *I-tsie-king-in-i* of Hiuen-ing, was composed about the year 649, in the section on *Mi-tsi-king-kang-li-cheu-king* (*sūtra* on the *Malla* or Licchavi). *Guhya-pada-vajra* (?) presents the follwing account.[2]

"*Yue-tchi*. It is the kingdom of *Pou-kia-lo* ; it is situated in the north-west of the mountain of Snows (Himalaya)." *Pou-kia-lo* (where *pou* is written with the same letter as in the above-mentioned word *lin pou se*) is undoubtedly *Pukkhalāvatī*. Puṣkarāvatī[3], mentioned as the capital of the *Yue-tchis* in the passages

1 Cf. Julien, *Methode*, 1503-1505, and the letters of the series *pou* in general ; *Ibid*, 1490-1518.

2 Chinese edition, Chap. 5, Korean edition, Chap. 4.

3 The most ancient capital of Gandhāra was Puṭkarāvati which is said to have been founded by Puṣkara, son of Bharata and nephew of Rāma (*Viṣṇupurāṇa*, Wilson's Ed., Vol. IV, Ch 4). Puṣkalāvati's antiquity is undoubted as it was the capital of an Indian prince named Hasti (Gk. Astes) at the time of Alexander's

that I have quoted.[1] The compiler Hiuen-ing has certainly reproduced a comment in the translation but I am not aware of the period when the translation of the *sūtra* was carried out, and even not aware which of the *sūtras* was involved. The Chinese collection and Japanese edition contain very clearly one *sūtra* under the same title : *Fo-jou-nie-pan mi-tsi-king-kang li-cheu ngai-lien-king*, translated in the Tsin period (350-431) ; but in fact, it concerns a differnt book. *Li-cheu-king* annotated by Hiuen-ing was in five chapters; in that book there was a description about the Yue-tchis, and also about the Iu-tiens (Khotan) and about the K'iu-tsis (Koutchi). There is no mention of these in the *Li-cheu-king* of our collections, which is, in addition, very brief.

The *Kiu-che-loun-soung-chou*, commentary on the *Abhidharma Koṣa*, mentions in the historic introduction the name of Kaniṣka (*Kia-ni-tcha-kia*) and quotes the interpretation given by Hoei-hoei, the learned commentator at the end of the twelfth century. Hoei-hoei, explains the name by *tsing kin che i.e.*, 'colour of pure gold'. I do not know if *Hoei-hoei* indicated in his book the authority of the tradition which he took into account in making the translation ; but I suspect that it was entirely his own work. However, it is interesting to state that the translation suits well to both the Sanskrit and Chinese forms of the name. An Indian etymologist would not feel any difficulty to hold that Kaniṣka is derived from the word *Kanaka*, 'gold'. On the other hand, the Chinese words (tsing) *kin-che*, "colour of gold (pure)" sounds like an echo of Kaniṣka. The word *kin* 'gold'is pronounced by the Cantonese as *kam*, and by the Japanese as *kin* and *kan* : it appears as *kum* in *Kumbhīra* to Hiouen-tsang and *kum* in *kambu*, 'shell'. The character *che*, 'colour' is pronounced by the Cantonese as *chik* and by the Japanese as *choka*. The Buddhist literature makes mention of a king 'of gold colour'; a special sūtra has been dedicated to him : the *Kin-che-wang-king* translatated in 542

---

expedition (326 B.C.). It is called Peukelaotis by Arrian and Peukalei by Dionysius Periegetes. During the reign of Maues (c. 75 B.C.) Puṣkalāvati came under the Śaka rule. Puṣkalāvati contained the royal residence of Kaniṣka's son (Smith, *Early History*, 4th Ed., p. 277, f. n. 1)—B. C. L.

1 *Journal Asiatique*, 1877, I, pp. 9 and 42.

by Gautama Prajñāruci; the original is to be found in the *Kanaka-varṇa-sūtra*[1], which forms the twentieth tale in the *Divyāvadāna* and which has been translated by Burnouf in his 'Introduction to the history of the Indian Buddhism' (pp. 90-98)[2]. If the interpretation given by Hoei-hoei is correct, or more or less conforms to the translation, it would be piquant to think that one could picture Kaniṣka in the image of the king Kanaka-varṇa, who was strength and charity personified.

It appears to me clearly from the texts that I have collected that the Buddhist authors and compilers of the seventh century have reproduced the information about the Buddha and the voyage of the king from *Wei-leao,* without taking any help of the extracts given in the annotations of *San-kouo-tchi.* We have then an independent tradition, based directly or indirectly on *Wei-leao*, or some intermediaries. Our quotations indicate at least the existence of two collections of texts, which though written about the same period, differ considerably, hence they could be used for checking each other.

A comparison of the two collections will enable us to solve the problem of the enigmatic king: In the year 2 before the christian era, a Chinese went to the country of the Yue-tchis; the king of the Yue-tchis communicated to him through his own son, the heir-apparent, some of the Buddhist texts. The Chinese, on returning to his country made them known to all. A comparison of the different works will not lead to any other interpretation.

After establishing this fact, we may try to follow the gradual modifications in the tradition. I have already in my first paper[3] referred to a passage from *Cheu-kia-fong-tchi* of Tao-siuen (650 A.D.)

---

1 *Divyāvadāna* (Cowell & Neil) pp 290-98. This story refers to the Buddha's stay at the Jetavana grove of Anāthapindika and to king Kanakavarṇa who was very opulent.—B. C. L.

2 See also Feer, *Avadānaśataka*, p. 119. The Avadānaśataka or the hundred *avadānas* translated into Chinese in the first half of the 3rd century A.D. and translated into French by L. Feer. Paris, 1897 and edited by J. S. Speyer (*Bibliotheca Buddhica*, III, St. Petersburg 1902-1909). Some narratives begin and end as in the *Avadānaśataka*—B. C. L.

3 *Journal Asiatique*, 1897, I, pp. 19-20.

INDEX